CONTENTS

SERIAL KILLERS
Encyclopedia

100 Short Stories
100 Serial Killers
1000's of Victims

ISBN-13 978-1494772161
ISBN-10 1494772167

Authored by

RJ Parker

RJ PARKER PUBLISHING

Edited by: Hartwell Editing
Cover design by: Aeternum Designs

License Notes

"This is a work of nonfiction. No names have been changed, no characters invented, no events fabricated."

RJ Parker

Monthly KINDLE HD FIRE Giveaway

***

Drawing each month on the 30th...

***

Enter to WIN
(No Purchase Necessary)

Click HERE   *http://www.rjparkerpublishing.com/*
Win-a-Kindle.html

INTRODUCTION

A serial killer, as originally described by Ronald Ressler of the FBI, is usually an individual (but may be a small group or an individual validated by a group) who murders three or more people over more than one event. The FBI recently changed this definition to an individual who commits two or more murders with a "cooling-off" period in which the killer plans and fantasizes about the next kill while reliving the previous one.

Ressler of the FBI's Behavioral Science Unit (BSU), used the term to describe a different class of killer who operates independently of criminal or political affiliation with an aim to take life due to personal reasoning, rather than any outside influence from society.

Serial killers usually kill for one of several reasons, including personal enjoyment, stress relief, or even to uphold a personal set of moral or rational values (such as the Yorkshire Ripper in the United Kingdom, who killed to clean the streets of what he believed to be a blight on his world).

Serial killers can come from a variety of socioeconomic backgrounds, can be male or female, and often have trouble empathizing with others.

***

The typical characteristics of a serial killer are hard to pin down; as there really aren't any concrete indicators beyond the simple fact that the individual has chosen to engage in a series of murders for his or her own reason. With that said, there are several broad trends that have been noted. Most specifically is the age range in which serial murderers become fully active—between the ages of twenty and forty. Older cases have been identified, but those are usually believed to be serial killers who avoided earlier detection. Younger people involved in serial killing have also been identified, but they are unlikely to be directly involved at first, and instead typically take a supporting role to a more dominant individual.

Serial killers are also typically male, although this view has been criticized in recent times, as female serial killers are not uncommon but still not as numerous as men. The major difference between male and female serial killers is in actual method, rather than motivation and capability. Women are more likely to choose passive methods, such as poisoning, while men tend to choose violent methods, such as strangulation or stabbing.

There are also a disproportionately high number of ethnic minority serial killers, especially in the U.S. This may be because they are more likely to succumb to an unstable, unusually stressful or abusive situation, due to the less than ideal treatment of ethnic minorities within many societies.

Serial killers are commonly thought of as intelligent, but recent research conducted in the United States has shown that they are in fact of average to below average intelligence, with an average IQ of 93. Many serial killers are often raised in abusive or unstable households and this abuse causes behavioural and mental problems later in life.

The Macdonald triad is a set of behavioural characteristics often used to describe the background and possible indications of a serial killer. This theory proposes that there are three behaviours common in serial killers. They include: a preoccupation and obsession with fire starting, a prevalence for sadistic behaviour as a child (which may involve the torture and killing of small animals), and bed wetting into the early teen years (past the age of twelve). However, there have always been exceptions to the above and a serial killer can emerge from any background or area of society.

***

The *modus operandi* (MO) is a term coined to refer to the particular methods and functional characteristics of a serial killer. The MO can be made up of different aspects, such as the time to strike, the characteristics of a victim, the tools to be used, the methods of gaining entry or luring and subduing a victim, or the locations used during the crime.

The MO can and often will be similar when conducted by the same person, as there are usually personal reasons or rational issues leading to the choice of a particular method. Similar MOs can be used to link homicides by police departments and possibly uncover an individual serial killer who may have gone unnoticed. The MO is similar to and may be involved in the signature of a particular serial killer, but the two are not one and the same. The signature is often a personal and symbolic feature of a serial killer's crimes and typically has personal meaning that may not be immediately apparent.

On the other hand, the MO also refers to the practical choices made by the serial killer in actually committing the act. Not all serial killers leave a signature, as not all murders may be 'perfect' or uninterrupted according to the killer. However, MOs will typically remain similar across all murders as the killer becomes comfortable with the act of killing. Analyzing MOs can be used to predict, link, and eventually convict serial killers by better understanding their methods and abilities. The motives of serial killers differ depending on their background and circumstances but can be put into one of four categories generally: visionary, mission-orientated, hedonistic and power seeking.

Visionaries believe an outside force compels them to commit murder. These outside forces are generally broken into two groups: demon spoken and God spoken. Those in the demon spoken group believe they are influenced by and led into the act due to an intangible force of evil intent that enjoys the act in some way. Those in the God spoken group believe they are led into the act due to a good or divine presence that justifies the act in terms of a higher power or greater good. Visionaries typically suffer from psychotic and hallucinatory breaks with reality, and are deemed mentally ill for the most part. They may be dealing with emotional trauma left over from an abusive or unusually stressful past.

Mission-orientated serial killers believe they are conducting some kind of service or fulfilling a function. This function is determined by the killer and his own ability to understand the world around him. They believe they are, in essence, conducting a mission, such a cleaning up the world or removing a perceived evil or problematic element of society (for example, prostitutes).

Hedonistic serial killers kill for the pleasure of killing and may also receive sexual gratification from the act. They kill for their own sexual pleasure and derive greater pleasure through greater depths of torture and mutilation. Hedonistic killers tend to increase the frequency of their attacks as they become more eager to repeat the process. They are also notorious for becoming sloppy and disregarding the possibility of being discovered.

Finally, power and control serial killers seek to kill in order to exercise some dimension of control over their victims. This includes the 'angel of death' cases, in which medical practitioners kill or attempt to kill patients in order to exercise power over who lives and who dies. These killers are also called thrill seeking killers, as they kill to get the thrill of dominance over their victims. Those who kill others for financial gain and material possessions also fall into this category, as the thrill of gaining something from someone else by murder is exercising the power and dominance over another person.

***

The following 100 stories are short (hence the title "Abridged"): two to three pages, and about 700 words each. It's a "Reader's Digest" of serial killers and an easy read. This would not be a book used for academic research. But, I promise that most of you will learn many things about these 100 killers.

There is also a bonus chapter at the end of this

book, written by up-and-coming true crime writer JJ Slate, on the Long Island Serial Killer. JJ's debut true crime book, *Missing Wives, Missing Lives*, a chilling collection of true cases in which a wife has mysteriously vanished, presumably at the hands of her husband, released June 16, 2014 and quickly became an Amazon bestseller in several categories.

For more details about JJ and her books, please visit any of the following sites:

Website

www.jenniferjslate.com

Facebook

www.facebook.com/jjslate

Twitter

www.twitter.com/jenniferjslate

CHAPTER 1:
AHMAD SURADJI

aka Nasib Kelewang

Claiming to be a witch doctor, many young girls and women would go to Ahmad's home and hire him to cast magic spells in hope of having better lives. They would request to be more attractive or wealthy, to find a successful future husband, or ask for spiritual or medical advice, while paying him in watches, jewelry and cash. An hourly session was $300. But, their better lives never came to be, as each one of them, all forty-two, were killed during the fake sessions.

Admad Suradji lived with his three wives, who all happened to be sisters, in Medan, the capital of North Sumatra in Indonesia. He was a cattle breeder who also practiced witchcraft, based on a dream he once had of his deceased father. He claimed that in this dream, the ghost of his father told him to kill seventy women and to drink their saliva so he could become a mystic healer. He built a reputation performing spells and healing the ill. Known by the villagers as Nasib Kelewang, people came from miles away and spent their savings hoping for a better life. Usually the girls wouldn't tell anyone where they were going, as they were embarrassed and thought nonbelievers would ridicule them. It was only by chance that one father knew about his daughter going to see Ahmad, and when she never returned, he notified the police.

That evening, on May 2, 1997, the police arrived on the sugarcane plantation and had a cursory look around the property, where they found the partial remains of a corpse. Ahmad and his three wives were taken in for questioning while a search of the property was conducted. After several hours of interviewing their suspect and his wives separately, he confessed. During his interrogation, three female bodies were unearthed on his property. He initially confessed to killing sixteen women over a span of five years, but days and weeks of searching the property revealed the personal effects of twenty-five missing women. Eventually, Admad admitted to killing forty-two girls and young women over some eleven years, from 1986 to 1997. The girls' ages ranged from eleven to thirty, many of them prostitutes. His wives were also arrested for accessory to murder. The forty-eight-year-old self-proclaimed mystic paranormal witch doctor obviously didn't predict his future correctly.

Getting back to the dream, Admad admitted during interrogation that he would bury the girls alive up to their waists and then strangle them with an electrical cord. He would drink their saliva, undress them, and then bury the victims with their heads pointing toward his house. He claimed his father told him in the dream that this would enhance his mystical powers. During the trial, he denied all of this and said that he had been tortured and coerced into confessing.

Five days shy of one year after being arrested, on

April 27, 1998, the high court in North Sumantra found the paranormal psychopath guilty of all forty-two killings, which amounted to a total of 363 charges. He was sentenced to death. Ahmad's wives were also initially sentenced to death for aiding in multiple homicides but their sentences were later reduced to life in prison after they agreed to testify against their husband.

For ten years, while authorities investigated other missing women in the country, they kept this serial killer alive in case they needed more answers. Finally, on July 10, 2008, he faced the firing squad, despite a last minute appeal from Amnesty International, a human-rights group.

CHAPTER 2: AILEEN WUORNOS

While prostitutes are usually an easy target for serial killers, this was not the case when it came to Aileen Wuornos. In less than a year, Wuornos, a prostitute herself, killed seven men. The story of her harsh criminal life began when she was just a teenager, and she later ended up being the first woman to fit the FBI's profile of a serial killer.

Aileen Carol Wuornos was born on February 29, 1956, to Diane Wuornos, who married Leo Dale Pittman (Aileen's father) when she was fifteen years old. Less than two years later, they got divorced. Pittman later turned out to be a child molester who died in 1969 by hanging himself in the prison, never meeting his daughter. Diane soon ran back to her parents where she abandoned her children, Keith and Aileen. The grandparents, Britta and Lauri Wuornos, legally adopted Aileen and her older brother Keith on March 18, 1960, and kept the truth from them. Growing up, Aileen had bursts of rage and anger. Learning the truth about her parents didn't help her unstable situation. Aileen and her brother soon became rebellious. She had sexual contact at an early age, even with her brother

Keith. At the age of fourteen, she became pregnant and gave birth to a boy who was ultimately given up for adoption. After her grandmother died of heart failure, Aileen's grandfather kicked her out of the house. Later, she ran away and picked up hitchhiking and prostitution. In 1976, while hitchhiking to Florida, Aileen met Lewis Gratz Fell, a sixty-nine-year-old who was the president of a yacht club. He fell in love with her, and they got married. However, she was still very violent, and was arrested a couple times because of her bar fights. Around six weeks later, Fell annulled the marriage after she hit him over the head with a bat. For the next decade, she jumped from one failed relationship to another. She was still working as a prostitute, engaging in criminal activities, and getting arrested for various offenses, such as driving under the influence, forgery, theft, and armed robbery. In 1986, she met twenty-four-year-old motel maid Tyria Moore, at a Daytona gay bar. They soon moved into an apartment together, where Aileen supported them through her prostitution.

Aileen began killing in 1989. She claimed that all the men she killed were ones that picked her up, and either beat her or raped her, so in self-defense, she shot them and disposed of their bodies. That was before she also robbed them.

· Her first victim was Richard Mallory (aged fifty-two years). His body was discovered on December 13, 1989, after an abandoned vehicle was discovered on December 1 and an investigation was opened. He was shot several times and killed by two bullets to his left lung.

- The body of the second victim, David Spears (aged forty-three years), was found on June 1, 1990, wearing only a baseball cap. Six bullets to the torso were the cause of his death.
- Charles Carskaddon (aged forty years) was Aileen's third victim. He was found dead on June 6, shot nine times in his lower chest and upper abdomen.
- Troy Burress (aged fifty years) was declared missing on July 31. Five days later, his decomposed body was discovered from a wooded place along the 19th State Road in Marion County. He was shot twice.
- On September 12, Charles Dick Humphreys (aged fifty-six), was also found dead, fully clothed, and shot six times in the torso and head.
- On November 19, the nearly nude body of Jeno Antonio (age sixty-two) was found. He was shot six times in the back and head. After five days, police also found his car in Brevard County.
- The last victim, Peter Siems, was never found. The sixty-five-year-old man was heading to New Jersey from Florida in June 1990. Law officers in Orange Springs found his car on July 4. Witnesses identified Aileen and her girlfriend Tyria Moore ditching the car. On the interior door handle, there was a print that matched Aileen's.

On January 9, 1991, Aileen Wuornos was arrested. The next day, Moore was located. Moore turned against Wuornos to help her clear her own name, and in order to help the police get a confession out of Wuornos. Aileen admitted murdering the men, but told investigators the reason was self-defense. Between January 1992 and February 1993, Wuornos was on trial. She was sentenced to six death sentences for the murders, with the exception of Peter Siems, since his body was never found. She resided on death row for almost ten years, and on October 9, 2002, she was executed by lethal injection.

CHAPTER 3: ALBERT HENRY DESALVO

aka The Boston Strangler

Many serial killers don't change their *modus operandi*, and they usual perfect their rituals, and in their minds, improve on each killing. The Boston Strangler was no different, and his last killing was by far his most brutal.

Young Albert DeSalvo had his first sexual experience at age six, and in that same year, aided his father in shoplifting and breaking and entering. "Monkey see, monkey do" is an accurate statement for this case. His father Frank was a mean and angry man. He was abusive to his wife and children, a raging alcoholic, and would put the fear of Christ in them for no reason. Frank once knocked out all of his wife's teeth and had broken every finger on her hands. He'd bring prostitutes into the home and have sex with them in front of the family.

By the time Albert commenced his serial raping and murdering, he was married and had his own children.

In June of 1962, the 'Strangler' killed his first victim, fifty-five-year-old Anna Sleser, whose body was discovered by her son on June 14, nude underneath her open housecoat and strangled with the cord of her evening gown. The crime was initially considered to be a breaking and entering gone badly that had ended in a homicide. Eighty-five-year-old Mary Mullen was killed in a similar way a couple weeks later. However, just two days after Mary was killed, two more seniors were discovered: Nina Nichols, age sixty-eight, and Helen Blake, age sixty-five, were both strangled with nylons. The authorities knew by this time that these killings were the work of one individual. At this time, they were unsure of a motive. Sometimes one person will kill multiple people to confuse police when their primary target was just one individual.

The murders ended shortly after they started when the Boston Strangler was arrested and sent to prison for rape. The police didn't realize at this time that they had also apprehended a serial killer.

His last victim was nineteen-year-old Mary Sullivan, whom he murdered when he broke into her apartment on January 4, 1964. He raped her at knifepoint and strangled her with his bare hands. He then posed the body to taunt the police. He placed a card reading "Happy New Year" between her toes, tied a silk scarf into a bow around her neck, spread her legs apart, and inserted a broom handle into her vagina.

DeSalvo was arrested for rape and sent to Bridgewater State Hospital for an evaluation. It was during this time that he boasted to other prisoners about the crimes he committed, and that he was the Boston Strangler. Most didn't take him seriously, but one inmate did and reported it to the now famous lawyer, F. Lee. Bailey, who was acting as DeSalvo's defense attorney. Bailey orchestrated a list of questions for the informant to ask DeSalvo, questions that only the real killer would know. After seeing the answers, there was no question in Bailey's mind that his client was the Boston Strangler.

Bailey took this information to the police but negotiated a deal so that they couldn't use DeSalvo's confession to press charges against him. The police accepted the deal, happy enough that the serial killer had been caught and was off the streets.

So, what was the motive of the Boston Stranger, who raped and killed thirteen females between the ages of nineteen and eighty-five? DeSalvo had a hypersexual disorder that even his wife couldn't satisfy five times a day. He murdered his victims after raping them so that he couldn't be identified.

In the end, DeSalvo was sentenced to life in prison for multiple rapes but no murder charges. He survived nine years before being shanked to death over a drug deal in Walpole State Prison on November 26, 1973.

CHAPTER 4: ALEXANDER PICHUSHKIN

The Bittsa Beast

Moscow had just celebrated the capture of serial killer Andrei Chikatilo and was in the process of a trial when Pichushkin "picked up the torch" and got his first taste of killing. This was in 1992. Alexander was just eighteen years old.

In a television confession years later, he admitted to pushing a teenage boy out the window of a moving car that year. He initially had told authorities that they boy jumped and it was suicide. "This first murder," he stated in the interview, "it's like first love, it's unforgettable." What caused him to kill once and then take a long cooling-off period is unknown. It's reported that he suffered a head injury when he was four years old and was hospitalized for a lengthy amount of time.

However, eight years later, in 2000, Pichushkin's grandfather had passed away and he fell into a deep depression. This is common in many serial killers: an emotionally altering event occurs that seems to ignite the reptile part of the brain. He would strike up conversations with homeless and elderly people at a nearby park, and would drink with them. He'd talk about his dog that he once had and how he buried the dog in the park. Then he'd show them where.

Many of the bodies were discovered in a nearby sewer pit and all were killed the same way: blunt-force trauma to the head using a heavy object, like a pipe or hammer. During the autopsies, it was apparent that some of his victims didn't die straight away but drowned in the sewage, as indicated by the contents in their lungs. Over the following months, the serial killer became more rushed and did not seem to care about being captured, which is typical of unorganized serial killers. They escalate their kills without planning or preparation.

Pichushkin took many chances: he killed at night, at day, and began leaving bodies lying around to be discovered sooner. He did not wear gloves to avoid fingerprints being left on weapons he'd use, such as alcohol bottles that he used to smash his victim's heads. He gave up using the sewer pit as his dumping grounds.

Over a three-year span, he killed over fifty people. Moscow residents were in a panic. With the exception of a couple of vague descriptions by two people who survived his beatings, authorities had very little to go on. The media dubbed him the 'Bittsa Beast,' named after the park where he committed his crimes, Bittsa Park.

On June 14, 2006, Marina Moskalyova, age thirty-six, would be the beast's last victim. She wrote a note for her son stating that she was going for a walk in the park with her supermarket co-worker, Alexander Pichushkin. He was not aware of the note. Although Marina was murdered, she probably saved many others by writing her son this brief message.

She was also carrying a train stub in her pocket, which led police to video footage of her and Pichushkin walking on the platform of the metro system just hours before she was murdered.

Pichushkin was picked up the next day and taken in for questioning. During the search of his flat, police discovered a chessboard. On the board, 62 out of 64 squares had dates written on them, and each date represented a different killing.

It is customary in Russia for a criminal to be filmed while reenacting his or her crimes. Parts of this documentary was aired on Russian television with Pichushkin explaining how he would lure the victim and hit him or her over the head from behind, so as to avoid blood castoff on himself. He said, "for me, a life without murder is like a life without food for you."

In the end, he was convicted of three attempted murder counts (as three people survived) and forty-nine murders, however, he very proudly asked to be charged with sixty murders. Judge Usov handed down a life sentence and ordered that the first fifteen years be spent in solitary confinement.

"Human life is not too long. It is cheaper than a sausage. My Lawyer: I would cut him open like a fish."
  - Alexander Pichushkin, March 13, 2008

Author's note: Read "An interview with a Russian Serial Killer" at The Exile - Interview with a Serial Killer with Yasha Levine.

CHAPTER 5: ALVIN & JUDITH ANN NEELLEY

Lisa Ann Millican was a sweet little girl with brown hair cut in shag that had a rough thirteen years of life. Born in 1969, she was sexually abused by her father for eleven years, until a social worker came to her rescue. She was removed from her family's home, and put in a home in Rome, Georgia, then transferred to the Harpst Home in Cedartown, Georgia. Before being placed in foster care, she had been living in a car with her mother and siblings. The night of September 25, 1982, while on a trip to Riverbend Mall, Lisa disappeared.

Judith Ann Adams Neelley was born in 1964. Her father died in an accident when she was just nine. Her mother would have her male companions come the family's trailer, and later was arrested for the contributing to the delinquency of a teenage boy. When she was fifteen, Judith met Alvin Howard Neelley, Jr., a car thief who was born in 1953. Soon, they couldn't imagine life without each other. Alvin was married, but decided to get a divorce and run away with Judith to Georgia in 1980. They were always on the move, robbing gas stations and convenience stores along the way from Georgia to Texas. Once, in 1980, they tried to rob a woman at gunpoint in the Riverbend Mall. They were eventually caught. Alvin was sent to prison for five years, and Judith was sent to the Youth Development Center (YDC). There, she gave birth to twins, and then transferred to a facility in Macon, Georgia. During that time, she wrote to Alvin claiming that she had been sexually abused in YDC. This made Alvin full of vengeance. When they got back together after their release, they decided to act upon their anger towards YDC. They shot at the house of Kenneth Dooley and threw a homemade Molotov cocktail at the residence of Linda Adairs (both staff members of YDC), after making threatening phone calls to both.

On September 25, 1982, Alvin and Judith abducted Lisa Ann Millican and kept her captive in different hotel rooms in Georgia and Alabama. For three days, they raped and tortured her, even in front of their children. They kept her handcuffed to the bed and forced her to sleep on the floor. Then Judith took her to a remote canyon in Alabama and tried to kill her by injecting her with drain cleaner products. When the first injection didn't kill her, she performed six more injections. The procedure was very painful, but Lisa still didn't die. That was when Judith shot Lisa in the back and head three times with a .38 pistol, and then shoved her over the edge of the cliff. Judith then called the police to report the incident while giving them instructions on where to find the body.

On October 4, 1982, Judith invited two strangers, John Hancock and his fiancée Janice Chatman, for a ride in her car. Then, Judith stopped and ordered John into the woods where she shot him. John survived, but his fiancée was not as lucky. Janice was taken back to the Neelleys' hotel room, where Alvin and Judith tortured, raped, and eventually shot her. Then they dumped the body in a wooded area nearby.

John identified his attackers to the police, who began searching for Alvin and Judith. Someone eventually recognized the couple on the police flyers that were distributed after the murder. On October 9, 1982, Judith was arrested, and Alvin was taken into custody a few days later. They both began blaming each other after they were taken into custody. John Hancock confirmed that they were his abductors, while Kenneth Dooley and Linda Adairs identified Judith's voice from the phone calls she had placed to their houses.

Alvin Neelley pled guilty to murder and assault, but he wasn't tried for the murder of Lisa Millican. Judith Neelley gave birth to her third child behind bars, and was tried in March 1983. She was convicted of Lisa Millican's murder and sentenced to death in Alabama's electric chair. She also pled guilty to the murder of Janice Chatman.

Alvin died in prison in November 2005. On January 15, 1999, Judith Neelley had her death sentence commuted to life in prison. She later became eligible for parole in January 2014. At the time of this writing, February 5, 2014, Judith had not yet applied for parole, but is expected to this year.

CHAPTER 6:
AMELIA DYER

Evelina Marmon was a popular twenty-five-year-old barmaid. In January of 1896, she gave birth to an illegitimate daughter she named Doris. She then placed an ad that simply read: "Wanted, respectable woman to take young child." Next to her ad was another: "Married couple with no family would adopt healthy child, nice country home. Terms $10." Marmon responded to the ad and received a reply. "Mrs. Harding," an older woman offered to take in the child while after insisting on the one-off payment. However, instead of taking care of the girl, "Mrs. Harding" and her twenty-three-year-old daughter killed Doris and used the money to pay the rent.

Amelia Dyer, who once used the alias "Mrs. Harding," was born in the small village of Pyle Marsh, east of Bristol. Her father, Samuel Hobley, was a master shoemaker. She learned to read and write, and she loved literature and poetry. However, her mother, Sarah Hobley née Weymouth, suffered from a mental illness caused by typhus. She cared for her mother and witnessed her violent fits. Sarah died in 1848. After her mother's death, Amelia lived with her aunt in Bristol before serving an apprenticeship with a corset maker. Her father died in 1859. When she was twenty-four, she became estranged from her siblings, and moved to Trinity Street, Bristol, where she met and married George Thomas (age fifty-nine). Two years later, she trained as a nurse, which was an exhausting but respectable job. Through contact with Ellen Dane, a midwife, she was introduced to a new way of earning a living: by using her home to provide for unmarried young pregnant women, and then farming off the babies for adoption or leaving them to die from neglect and malnutrition. The profession (baby farming) was common, since unmarried pregnant women in Victorian England often struggled. Regular or single payments were made to the caregiver to take care of the pregnant women until they gave birth, and then care for the unwanted babies.

Dyer advertised in the newspaper and meet with the clients, while assuring them that she was married, respectable, and would do her best to provide for the child. The parents thought they were leaving their babies in a safe and loving home. Then, Dyer would let the children die from starvation until it became inconvenient for her, at which point she began murdering them.

In 1879, a doctor became suspicious about the high death rate of children in Dyer's care. She was caught, but instead of being convicted of murder, she was only sentenced to six months of hard labour for neglect. When she was released, she tried to return to her nursing career. When she needed to disappear due to suspicion, she would get admitted to a mental hospital with alleged mental instability and suicidal tendencies. Since she had worked as an asylum nurse, she knew what to do to seem mentally ill.

Later, she returned to baby farming, and murdering children again for profit. This time, she got rid of the bodies herself because she didn't want to involve the doctors for death certificates, which raised more suspicion. She and her family always seemed to be relocating since the police and parents wanting their babies back were drawing attention to her activities.

On March 30, 1896, a bargeman retrieved a package from the Thames at Reading. It contained the body of baby Helena Fry. Detective Anderson used microscopic analysis of the wrapping paper and found the name Mrs. Thomas and an address. This led the police to Dyer. After collecting additional evidence, the police raided the home of Dyer on April 3. They found much more evidence connecting her to the murder. The next day Dyer was arrested and charged with murder.

On May 22, 1896, Amelia Dyer pleaded guilty for the murder of Doris Marmon before the Old Bailey. Her defense was insanity, but the prosecutor argued that she knew what she was doing was wrong. The jury found her guilty after only four and a half minutes. She spent three weeks in the condemned cell. On Wednesday, June 10, 1896, she was hanged.

Her son-in-law was charged as accomplice, but the charges against her daughter were dropped. Although being convicted for just one murder, Amelia Dyer had killed more than 400 children over the period of twenty years.

CHAPTER 7: ANATOLY ONOPRIENKO

In 1989, two intruders went into a house to rob it. Sergei Rogozin was a gym patron who had already robbed many other homes with Anatoly Onoprienko. This time was different. During the robbery, a family of ten stumbled upon the men. The weapons carried by the two men for self-defense were used in murdering the family of two adults and eight children. After that incident, Onoprienko cut off all contact with Rogozin, but his thirst for blood and revenge did not end. After some time, the killings continued.

The story started around thirty years ago. Anatoly Onoprienko was born on July 25, 1959, in the town of Lasky in Zhytomyr Oblast, Ukraine. At the age of four, his mother passed away. The death of his mother had a huge impact on his life, since he was handed to an orphanage in the village of Privitnoe soon afterwards. He resented the fact that his father gave him away but still cared for his older brother. He grew up and studied forestry, but still felt angry over the injustice of being pulled away from his family. Later, he started acting upon this anger by committing his first murder in 1989, and many other murders in the years to come.

A few months after killing the family of ten, Anatoly Onoprienko was planning to burglarize a car. Unfortunately, he found five people, including an eleven-year-old boy, sleeping in the car. Onoprienko shot them to death and burned their bodies. The killing streak would then continue on for six more years.

On December 24, 1995, another robbery turned out to be an opportunity for murder. At Garmarnia, a village in central Ukraine, Onoprienko tried to rob the Zaichenko family of four. He was carrying a double-barreled shotgun, which he used to kill the four members of the family before setting the place on fire. A few days later, on January 2, another family of four was murdered. This time Onoprienko also killed a male pedestrian that spotted him to eliminate any possible witnesses. The murders were becoming more frequent. On January 6, on the Berdyansk-Dnieprovskaya highway, Onoprienko stopped cars and killed the drivers. Four people were killed that day: a Navy ensign, a kolkhoz cook, a taxi driver, and an unidentified victim. Eleven days later, Onoprienko shot and murdered the Pilat family of five in their home, which he then set on fire. Onoprienko also killed a fifty-six-year-old pedestrian (Zakharo) and a twenty-seven-year-old railroad worker (Kondzela) because they could have witnessed the murder. The killing spree continued on January 30, when Onoprienko shot a woman (Marusunia), her two kids, and a visitor (Zagranichniy, thirty-two years old) in the Kievskaya Oblast region of Ukraine. These were his first thirty-nine victims.

On February 19 of the same year, Onoprienko

broke into the house of the Dubchak family in Olevsk, Zhitomirskaya Oblast. There, he shot the father and the son first. Then, with a hammer, he mauled the mother to death. He demanded money from the daughter, and when she refused, he also mauled her to death. On February 27, another family, the Bodnarchuks, was murdered in their home in Malina, Lvivskaya Oblast. Onoprienko shot the parents and then killed the daughters with an axe; the girls were aged seven and eight. Their neighbour, a businessman named Tsallk, was nearby. Onoprienko also killed him by shooting and then hacking up his corpse. His last victims were members of the Novosad family, whom he shot on March 22, 1996 and then set their home ablaze.

In March 1996, Onoprienko was captured after moving in with a relative where his weapons were found, along with souvenirs he took from his victims. He escaped the death penalty, since Ukraine had entered the Council of Europe, and instead was sentenced to life imprisonment. On August 27, 2013, Onoprienko died of heart failure at the age of fifty-four.

Onoprienko murdered fifty-two people in just six to seven years. He claimed that inner voices commanded him to kill. He always chose isolated houses, killed adult males first, then the rest of the family, and then set the house on fire to eliminate any possible witnesses. No wonder he was called "The Beast of Ukraine," "The Terminator," and "Citizen O."

CHAPTER 8: ANDREI ROMANOVICH CHIKATILO

One of the cruelest series of outrageous crimes happened in the Russian SFSR, the Ukrainian SSR, and the Uzbek SSR in a period that ranged from 1978 to 1990. The killer was estimated to be from twenty-five to fifty years old, a man suffering from sexual inadequacy, and a sadist who found relief in the cruelty of his crimes. He blinded his victims so they wouldn't look at him. Most of the murders were committed in Rostov Oblast, thus he was called the Rostov Ripper, the Butcher of Rostov, and the Red Ripper.

Andrei Romanovich Chikatilo was born in Ukraine during the Stalin era, at the time of a famine caused by crop failures and Stalin's collectivization of agriculture, and cannibalism circulated. When he was young, his mother told him that his elder brother was abducted, murdered, and cannibalized by ravenous neighbours; however, this story was never confirmed. He wasn't able to control his bladder and seminal emission due to brain damage that he had been born with, and was often beaten by his mother for wetting the bed.

During his teenage years, he was a model student and an enthusiastic Communist. He graduated with excellent grades in 1954. He discovered that he suffered from chronic impotence. He spent some years serving in the army. He eventually married Feodosia Odnacheva, and had two children with her: a boy and a girl. He started teaching the Russian language and literature, but his teaching career ended in March 1981, when he was charged with child molestation of both sexes.

His first documented murder was the killing of a nine-year- old girl, Yelena Zakotnova. He lured the girl to a house he had secretly purchased. He tried to rape her but could not get an erection, and when she struggled to escape, he choked her and stabbed her in the abdomen three times. He then threw her body into a river, where she was discovered two days later. Although there was so much evidence linking Chikatilo to the murder, another man named Aleksandr Kravchenko was actually captured, tried, and executed for her murder. Chikatilo continued murdering, finding he could only become sexually aroused and achieve orgasm while killing.

He killed both males and females; he wasn't particular. For the women or girls, he would destroy the vagina, uterus, bladder, and sometimes abdomen. He would also rip out their breasts. Once, he chewed off the nipple of a victim. For the men or boys, he mutilated the penis, scrotum, and anus, sometimes postmortem. He stabbed some victims in the eyes, because he believed that the image of what they last saw would be saved.

Over a period of twelve years, Chikatilo killed, mutilated, tortured, and sometimes ate more than fifty innocent people. Their ages ranged from seven to forty-five years old. His last victim was Svetlana Korostik, a twenty-two-year-old woman. He cut up pieces of her and ate them.

The lead detective in the investigation was Viktor Burakov. He suspected that the killer was luring his victims at the train station, so he put undercover officers there to keep watch. Next to the Donleskhoz train station, a man previously arrested and interrogated was discovered in the wooded area with little branches on his coat and red spots on his cheek; it was Andrei Chikatilo. Not far from that location, a victim was found slaughtered and mutilated. Chikatilo was detained and confessed to the murders during questioning. His motive was finding sexual relief after killing, something he couldn't achieve during intercourse while the victim was alive.

Chikatilo was found to be sane, and therefore stood trial. He was charged and convicted of fifty-two murders and sentenced to death. During the trial, he was kept in an iron cage to keep him safe from the families of the victims. Judge Leonid Akhobzyanov declared, "Taking into consideration the monstrous crimes he committed, this court has no alternative but to impose the only sentence that he deserves. I therefore sentence him to death." He was executed in February of 1994. He confessed to a total of fifty-six murders.

CHAPTER 9: ÁNGEL RESENDIZ

Ángel Resendiz is a living confirmation to the saying: "Size doesn't matter." Standing just 5'7" tall, he surely struck a lot of terror in the States, mainly in Texas. He wasn't a tall man, and his ways were primitive. However, he was still able to take the lives of at least fifteen victims.

Ángel Leoncio Reyes Recendiz was born on August 1, 1960, in Matamoros, Mexico. His mother didn't marry his father, and often physically abused him. At age six, he was sent to his uncle who sexually abused him. At eleven, he ran away and started living on the street where he began sniffing glue.

He first attempted to enter the U.S. through Texas when he was sixteen years old. However, he was deported. Over the years, he tried to get into the U.S. illegally many times and was always deported. He spent eleven years of his adult life in and out of American prisons where he served time for various crimes, including auto theft, burglary, assault, and even firearm possession. At the time of his final arrest, he was married and had a daughter.

Ángel would pick his victims randomly when he was traveling by train. He would attack them near railways and use objects to bludgeon them to death. He raped some of the female victims. He would also steal valuables from his victims. He usually covered his victims with a blanket or other item when he was finished with them.

Ángel's first known murder was in 1986, when he shot an unidentified homeless woman and her boyfriend with a .38 caliber gun. On July 19, 1991, Ángel bludgeoned thirty-three-year-old Michael White to death using a brick. On March 23, 1997, he used an air hose coupling to bludgeon nineteen-year-old Jesse Howell to death. Ángel also raped Jesse's sixteen-year-old fiancée, Wendy Von Huben, strangled her, and suffocated her with his hands.

On August 29, 1997, he attacked twenty-one-year-old Christopher Maier and his girlfriend, Holly Dunn Pendleton, while they were taking a walk near the railroad tracks. Christopher was hit to death with a rock, and Holly was raped and beaten, but miraculously survived and went on to help other rape victims.

On October 4, 1998, Ángel broke into the house of Leafie Mason (age eighty-one) through a window. He used a flat iron to beat her to death. On December 17, 1998, thirty-nine-year-old Claudia Benton was murdered. Ángel raped, stabbed, and bludgeoned her to death. His fingerprints were found at the scene and a warrant was issued for his arrest, but only for burglary.

On May 2, 1999, Ángel used a sledgehammer to bludgeon Norman J. Sirnic (age forty-six) and Karen Sirnic (age forty-seven) to death. His fingerprints were also found at the scene. On June 4, Noemi Dominguez (age twenty-six) was bludgeoned to death. On the same day, Josephine Konvicka (age seventy-three) was killed with the same pickaxe that Ángel used to kill Noemi. Josephine was sleeping when she received the killing blow.

On June 15, 1999, George Morber, Sr. (age eighty) was shot with a shotgun and Carolyn Frederick (age fifty-two) was killed with a tire iron. Ángel is suspected to have committed other murders as well, and he eventually confessed to seven more in Mexico.

The police were already leading an investigation on the murders, and they knew that they were looking for Ángel since he had left his fingerprints at the scene of multiple crimes. The FBI was brought in, and Ángel was placed on their Top Ten Most Wanted List, with a reward increasing from $50,000 to $125,000 in just few days. They knew that after the last murder, Ángel was hiding in Mexico.

Texas Ranger Drew Carter reached out to Ángel's beloved sister, Manuela. He promised her that if Ángel surrendered he would be put safely in jail, allowed to have visitors, and have access to psychiatric help. The deal was put into writing. On July 13, 1999, Drew, Manuela, and her pastor all met on the bridge between Zaragosa, Mexico, and El Paso. Ángel surrendered to Drew. On May 17, 1999, he was found guilty of first-degree murder, and received the death sentence. On June 27, 2006, he was executed by lethal injection.

CHAPTER 10: ANNA MARIA ZWANZIGER

"It is perhaps better for the community that I should die, as it would be impossible for me to give up the practice of poisoning people." These were some of the last words of Anna Maria Zwanziger, the mysterious housekeeper who called arsenic her "truest friend."

Anna Schonleben was born in in Nuremberg, Germany in 1760. Her father was an innkeeper, though her parents died when she was very young. She later married Zwanziger, a tough poor man. Anna read to provide an escape from her unhappy marriage. At the age of twenty-one, she inherited a property that her parents left her. Her husband helped her spend all the money on glamorous balls and carousals and when the money came to an end, their former mode of life continued. The husband lived in the wine-house, and she lived alone. They got lucky again when Zwanziger won a prize in the lottery. Again, there were songs and dances in the house until there was no more money.

Her husband died of alcoholism in 1776, and her fortune declined until she was forced to become a servant. She took orders from her employers, but neglected them. Soon, she was out of a job. She tried to get back with one of her lovers, and attempted suicide twice to get his attention, but was sent away. Later, she took an exhausting job in Vienna to a family of a Mr. Von S. However, she quit her job, taking with her one piece of jewelry. She advertised and moved to a small town called Neumarkt, and changed her name to Nanette Schonleben.

Schonleben's murderous life began at age forty, when she was working for a judge named Glaser. At the time, she was trying to find a husband to re-establish herself. Although Glaser was separated from his wife, Frau, they were still married. Schonleben did all she could to convince him to get back with his wife, and she succeeded. However, within four weeks of her return, Frau fell terminally ill and died. Shortly after, Nannette transferred herself to the service of a twenty-eight-year-old gentleman residing in Sanspareil, named Grohmann. Nannette came to service him with the best of recommendation from Glaser. Grohmann suffered from frequent fits of gout. She stayed at his side and tried to win his heart, but he decided he wanted another woman for a wife. He made advances to a lady, and proposed. Just before the marriage, Grohmann fell terminally ill and died.

Highly recommended, she found a new home. She was sent to take care of a pregnant woman by the name Gebhard. Nannette took care of her, and the child was born. After three days, the woman became ill, wouldn't cease vomiting, and after much endured pain, died. The baby was left in the care of Nannette. She remained a servant at the house, where some of the other servants also fell ill. On September 1, 1809, there was a large party in the house of Mr. Gebhard, and the people who had attended became sick after drinking beer served by Nannette. Everyone urged Mr. Gebhard to let her go, and he was obliged to do so. Before going, she expressed grief, filled the saltcellar with her own hands, and had a cup of chocolate with her master to say goodbye. Soon after her departure, those who drank the chocolate prepared by Nannette fell ill and began vomiting.

Through the examination of the salt barrel in Mr. Gebhard's house, an amount of arsenic was found. In October, 1809, Mr. Gebhard had Nannette arrested. She seemed the most innocent creature, but underneath was an unimagined evil. Her trial was on April 16, 1810. At first, she denied everything. However, when she learned that arsenic was found in victims' stomachs, she confessed. At the time of her trial and conviction, she was fifty years old.

She admitted that the arsenic had become an object of passion to her. She often poisoned her employers and brought them back to health to gain their affection. She was beheaded in July of 1811, and died without repentance.

CHAPTER 11: ARTHUR GARY BISHOP

"Come with me, I will give you free candy." This was how Arthur Gary Bishop lured Alonzo Daniels, a four-year-old boy, into his apartment where he sexually assaulted him. Then he drowned him in the bathtub, and buried the boy's little lifeless body in the desert. Bishop's first murder occurred on October 14, 1979; he waited approximately one year before killing again. During a period of four to five years, Arthur Bishop molested and murdered five young boys all between the ages of four and thirteen.

Bishop was born in Hinckley, Utah. He had five younger brothers. He was raised as a devout Mormon. Growing up, Arthur Bishop was an honour student, and an Eagle Scout as well. At the age of eighteen, he served as a missionary in the Philippines. That is why it was a surprise to most when, in February 1978, Arthur was arrested for embezzlement. He was given a five-year suspended sentence, but instead he skipped his parole and began living in Salt Lake City under the name of Roger Downs. He was excommunicated from the LDS Church in October 1978. Under the name of Roger Downs, Bishop joined the "Big Brother" program. He was not suspected of child molestation, but after he was later arrested, several children accused him of sexual assault.

One year after his first murder, Bishop struck again. In November 1980, he met an eleven-year-old boy named Kim Peterson at a skating rink, and offered to buy a pair of roller-skates from him. Then, in his apartment, he beat the boy to death with a hammer, and buried his body next to his first victim, Alonzo Daniels. Witnesses around the skating rink gave a description of the man last seen with Kim: a white male between twenty-five and thirty years old, around 200 pounds, and with dark hair. Bishop was brought in and questioned by the police, but not considered a suspect.

He killed his third victim, four-year-old Danny Davis, on October 20, 1981. This time, he lured and took the boy from a supermarket to his nearby home. There were several witnesses shopping in the area who were able to give a vague description of the man seen with the boy, and even agreed to go under hypnosis in order to remember more details. A huge search was launched as teams combed nearby fields, mountains, ponds, and lakes. The FBI was contacted and a $20,000 reward was offered. The boy was never found.

On June 23, 1983, he abducted six-year-old Troy Ward from a local park near Bishop's home. There were witnesses who saw the boy leaving with a man, but they couldn't provide a detailed description of him to police. Bishop sexually assaulted Troy, bludgeoned him, and then drowned him in the bathtub.

Arthur Bishop's final kill happened a month later,

on July 14. Thirteen-year-old Graeme Cunningham went camping with a friend and an adult chaperone, which unfortunately was Arthur Bishop. The boy never came back.

While leading the investigation, the police noticed that Bishop, under the alias of Roger Downs, lived in the neighbourhood where the murders had occurred, and even knew the fifth boy's parents. He was brought in for questioning regarding the disappearance of Graeme Cunningham. At the station, the police discovered Bishop's real name, and got a full confession out of him for all five murders. Bishop stated that he would do it again because he had gotten a thrill when he committed his murders.

Bishop attributed the killings to the fact that he had become addicted to child pornography and had fantasized about it so much that he felt compelled to act his fantasies out. He was brought to trial on February 27, 1984, found guilty of five counts of aggravated murder, kidnapping, and one count of sexually abusing a minor. He was sentenced to death by lethal injection upon his request. Before his death, he apologized to the victim's families.

CHAPTER 12: BEVERLEY ALLITT

The children's unit in Grantham Hospital, Ward 4, was struck by several unexpected sudden deaths, over a period between February and April of 1991. In just fifty-nine days, four children were murdered and six suffered serious body harm. The link between all of them was Nurse Beverly Allitt.

Beverly Allitt was a caring and devoted nurse. No one knew that under the mask she wore, Allitt was a serial killer. Since adolescence, Beverly Allitt had always been an attention seeker. She was shown to be typical of Munchausen Syndrome, a condition in which she would claim she was ill or cause herself to fall ill. When her constant attempts in getting more attention did not work, she began inflicting damage upon others to get attention. Her odd behaviour was obvious during her training in a nursing home. Later on, to draw more attention to herself, she would wear bandages and casts over wounds that she wouldn't allow anyone to examine.

Her first victim was seven-month-old Liam Taylor. Baby Liam was admitted to the ward with a chest infection on February 21, 1991. Allitt reassured the parents that he was receiving the best care possible and persuaded them to go home and rest. While the parents were gone, Liam suffered a respiratory emergency, but recovered. Allitt volunteered to watch over Liam another night. Just before midnight, the boy suffered from another respiratory crisis, but recovered again. Whenever left alone with Allitt, Liam's condition would worsen. Eventually, the boy suffered cardiac arrest and severe brain damage under Allitt's care. He was able to remain alive only with the help of the life support machines. The baby was eventually removed from life support after his parents made the decision based on medical advice. Allitt was never questioned.

Her second victim was Timothy Hardwick, who was admitted on March 5, 1991, following an epileptic seizure. He was left under Allitt's care, and died despite the efforts of the emergency resuscitation team. The autopsy was unable to provide a clear reason of death, thus blaming it on his epilepsy.

Allitt's third victim was one-year-old Kayley Desmond, who had been admitted due to a chest infection. On March 8, Kayley suffered cardiac arrest while under Allitt's care. This time the resuscitation team successfully revived her, and Kayley was then transferred to another hospital. There they discovered a puncture hole under her armpit and an air bubble near the puncture mark, but no one investigated it further. Had she not been transferred, it is likely she would have died as well.

Her next victim was Paul Crampton, a five-month-old baby. Allitt was caring for the patient alone when he suffered from insulin shock, which almost put him in a coma three times. The fluctuation in his insulin levels could not be explained, and he was taken to another hospital where he too recovered.

Later, Beverly Allitt attempted to murder five-year-old Bradley Gibson and two-year-old Yik Hung Chan, but was twice unsuccessful. Unfortunately, two-month-old Becky Phillips was not so lucky. Her twin sister, Katie Phillips, lived, but suffered from permanent partial paralysis, partial blindness, and brain damage due to oxygen deprivation caused by Allitt. Ironically, the mother of the twins asked Allitt to be the godmother due to her care for the girls. Her last victim was Claire Peck, a fifteen-month-old who suffered cardiac arrest twice under Allitt's care and died the second time.

After Claire's death, the police were summoned to investigate these suspicious incidents. It was found that Allitt was the nurse on duty during all the attacks and had access to the drugs. She was charged with four counts of murder, eleven counts of causing bodily harm, and eleven counts of attempted murder, to which she pled not guilty. On May 28, 1993, she was found guilty of all charges and sentenced to thirteen concurrent life terms. The judge recommended that she serve a minimum term of thirty years, and not be released until she was no longer considered a danger to the public. This was one of the longest sentences ever given to a woman in Britain at the time. She is currently serving her sentence at Rampton Secure Hospital in Nottinghamshire.

CHAPTER 13: BLOODY BENDERS

The year was 1870, and the Bender family of four had just moved to Kansas, in the area where the house that inspired *The Little House on the Prairie* was situated. They were Spiritualists. This religion was foreign to the homesteaders in the state. Mr. and Mrs. Bender mostly spoke German or heavily accented English, while the son and daughter spoke fluent English. Their one-room house was divided into two areas: the family quarters at the back of the house, and a public inn and store in the front. This family was later to be known as the Bloody Benders, whose real fate was never known.

Little is known about the Bender family before they settled in Kansas, near the Great Osage Trail in 1870. John Bender, Sr., called "Pa," claimed the 160 acres of land, in what now is called Labette County. His son John claimed a smaller parcel. The family also included of "Ma," and a daughter named Kate.

Later investigations revealed that none of them were actually named Bender. Only Ma and Kate were really related. Pa was born in 1870 as John Flickinger, in either Netherland or Germany. Ma was Almira Meik, who was first married to a Griffith and had twelve children with him. Before marrying Pa, she had married several other men who had all mysteriously died from a head wound. Kate was born as Eliza Griffith; she was attractive, and claimed to have psychic abilities, which drew more customers to their Inn. John Bender, Jr. was born John Gebhart, and it was believed that he was actually Kate's husband, not brother.

Many men passed through Kansas on their way to the West. Some were never heard from again. Since they were mostly adventurous travelers, their disappearances didn't draw much attention because it was normal for them to be out of touch. However, over the years, many persons went missing when they passed through Labette County. Bodies were eventually found, but no one knew who had committed the murders.

It turned out that the guests at the Inn were asked to sit in the place of the honour, against the separating curtain. While having dinner, from behind the curtain, someone would hit the guest in the head, slit his throat, and then drop the body through a trap door under his chair that led to the cellar. One traveller, Mr. Wetzell, later recalled that when he had stayed at the Inn and refused to sit in the guest of honour chair, Ma had become angry and abusive. He and his companion left when they saw the male Benders come from behind the curtain. Another man, William Pickering, told the same story.

In 1872, George Loncher had lost his wife and made plans to move from Kansas to settle in Iowa with his infant daughter. They never arrived at their destination. Dr. William York began searching for them, and on his way back home, he also disappeared. Dr. York's two powerful brothers, Colonel Ed York and Kansas Senator, Alexander York, began their own investigation, questioning the people of Labette County. In Harmony Grove, the township held a meeting in which the male Benders were present, and they decided to search each home for evidence. Unfortunately, the weather took a turn for the worse and it was several days before the search could begin. One neighbour noticed that the Bender's Inn was empty, and it was discovered that they were gone, along with their wagon. When the search team looked in the Bender's Inn, blood was discovered in the cellar. The garden was dug up, and the body of Dr. York was found. In the Bender farm, ten bodies were found with their skulls bashed in and throats cut. There was even the mutilated body of a girl around eight years old. Twenty-one murders were attributed to the Benders. In addition, the Bender family had stolen about $4,600 from their victims.

The Benders were never actually found, although a reward was offered to the public. Some women were arrested but they could not be positively identified as Ma or Kate. Many myths surrounded the Bender family, but their true whereabouts was never discovered, and after 144 years, no one knows what happened to them.

CHAPTER 14: BRUNO LDKE

One of the biggest murder mysteries in history surrounds the mystery of Bruno Lüdke, an alleged serial killer from Germany with more than eighty victims. He is believed to be one of Europe's deadliest serial killers. The murders were believed to have begun in 1928, and continued for a period of fifteen years. This was a time of economic and political chaos in Germany, which made it easier for people to disappear. His victims were mostly women. Lüdke was actually well known by the police as a thief and a peeping Tom at the time. However, he had a mild intellectual disability, which made it harder to believe that he could go on all these years killing and still be undetected by the police.

At a young age, Lüdke found pleasure in killing animals. Later, when he was eighteen years old, he began killing humans. During the war, Lüdke was caught by the police after molesting a young woman and was sterilized under the Gestapo leader Heinrich Himmler's orders. Most of his murders occurred in the years before World War II. He would stalk women and then rape, stab, and strangle them, sometimes even raping them again after murdering them. Even after his sterilization, nothing would stop him from continuing his murderous career.

On January 31, 1943, in the woods near Köpenick, a fifty-nine-year-old widow, Frieda Rössner, was found dead after being strangled with her shawl. Her purse was missing and she showed signs of post-mortem sexual abuse. On March 1943, the police brought Lüdke in for questioning. He tried to assault the police when he was asked if he had anything to do with Rössner's murder, and he was arrested. Bruno Lüdke then confessed to the murder, along with approximately eighty other murders. He claimed that his main reason for committing the murders was sexual gratification. He never faced trial for any of his crimes. Instead of prosecuting him, he was declared insane by the Nazis, and was sent to the Institute of Criminological Medicine in Vienna to be a human guinea pig. There, he underwent many medical experiments until he died on April 8, 1944, when an experiment involving chemicals proved to be deadly.

The confession he made after being arrested was enough for the police to blame him for the deaths of more than fifty-one women. What is puzzling about his story was that he was an intellectually disabled man who could not even tell investigators how many minutes there were in an hour, yet he seemed to have been able to commit scores of murders without ever being caught. In addition, during all these years, no one had ever really complained about Lüdke's behaviour. None of the crime scenes showed similarities or signatures, which could have indicated that different killers had committed the murders. In addition, no fingerprints or evidence against this allegedly notorious serial killer were found. There were many claims that the police were careless, and their reports were inconclusive and vague. Some criminologists state that the police had forced Lüdke's confessions. I personally think that he was above average intelligence to have been so organized and he eluded the police by changing his MO.

Some believe that Bruno Lüdke was a deadly serial killer, while others claim that he was just someone the police used to pin the murders on. Sometimes, it seems hard to believe that someone with a mental disability would be able to commit such crimes and get away with it, and at the same time evade the authorities for years. However, due to the period in which the crimes occurred, when it was so easy for someone to get away with murder, we can never be sure. The murders remain unsolved today. Was it the work of Bruno? I believe he had fun taunting the authorities and simply may have pretended to be of low intellect.

CHAPTER 15: CAROL M. BUNDY

Carol Bundy and her lover and accomplice, Doug Clark, eventually came to be known as "the Sunset Strip Killers." The notorious couple was convicted of many vicious murders that occurred in Los Angeles during late spring to early summer of 1980.

Carol Bundy had a difficult childhood. Her mother died when she was still young, and her father abused her after his wife's death. Although she was constantly abused, she still idolized her father. She convinced herself that he beat her because he wanted the best for her and her siblings. Her martyrdom would draw the path of her life, as she grew attached to every man she was with despite the fact that they were using her. When her father got married again, she was sent to a foster home. At the age of seventeen, she married a man thirty-nine years her senior. She wouldn't meet Doug Clark until she was thirty-seven years old, escaping a third abusive marriage with two young sons. She became infatuated with John Murray, her apartment manager who was also a part-time country singer. She started having an affair with him in the hopes that he would soon leave his wife. She even tried to bribe his wife into leaving him. Still, John wouldn't leave his family for Carol. Even after she was evicted, she kept frequenting places where Murray was performing. In one of the bars, Little Nashville, she met Doug Clark and they moved in together. The couple discovered that they both had similar dark sexual fantasies.

Clark began to bring prostitutes back home to have sex with both of them. Later, he told Bundy about his desire to kill a girl during sex. On his demand, Bundy bought two automatic guns for Clark. One night in June 1980, when Clark came home he was covered in blood. He told Bundy that he had killed two teenagers by shooting them in the head after he had ordered them to perform fellatio. Then he had raped their bodies. The next day, the bodies were found near the Ventura Freeway, where he had dumped them. Bundy was startled by the news, and anonymously provided the police with some information about the murders but she still protected Clark's identity. Twelve days later, Clark lured two prostitutes, Karen Jones and Exxie Wilson, into his car, shot them, and dumped their bodies. This time he took Exxie Wilson's head as a souvenir and stored it in the fridge at home. Bundy applied make up to the Exxie's face so that Clark could use it for necrophilia. Two days later, they dumped the head. Clark's first victim, a runaway named Marnette Comer, was found three days later. Clark would then wait a month before killing again. These were not the only victims of Doug Clark.

Meanwhile, Bundy was still attending John Murray's shows. One time, after a few drinks, she told Murray about what was going on with Clark. In order to stop him from telling the police, Bundy lured him to the van to have sex, and killed him by shooting and decapitating him. This showed how much Clark had an influence on Carol Bundy. But people had seen her leaving the bar with Murray, and two days later, Bundy confessed to her co-workers. She later gave a full confession for the crimes she committed with Clark.

Clark was arrested after Bundy's confession, and he was found in possession of the guns used in the murders. Bundy was convicted for two murders, John Murray and an unknown victim, while Clark was convicted for six murders. Clark tried to blame Bundy for the murders. However, the jury did not believe him, and in 1983, he was sentenced to death. Bundy pleaded guilty. Since she testified, she was only sentenced to life imprisonment. On December 9, 2003, Bundy died in prison from heart failure. She was sixty-one years old. Clark still resides on death row.

CHAPTER 16: CARIL ANN FUGATE

Once upon a time, a boy fell in love with a girl. The girl liked him back, and soon they started dating. One day, the girl came back home to find that the boy had shot her stepfather and mother, and stabbed and strangled her baby sister. Then, the girl and the boy went on a killing spree together. This is the story of Caril Fugate and Charles Starkweather.

Caril Ann Fugate was born on July 30, 1943. She lived with her mother and stepfather in Lincoln, Nebraska. In 1956, Caril was thirteen years old. Her sister, Barbara, had started a relationship with Bob von Busch, who introduced his friend, Charles Starkweather, to Caril. Although Charles was five years older than Caril, they began dating. Charles was a high school dropout, the third of seven children. He was born on November 24, 1938, to Guy and Helen Starkweather. His family was poor and uneducated, but hardworking. He worked unloading trucks at the Western Newspaper Union warehouse.

After the incident on January 21, 1958, when Charles murdered Caril's family, the couple stayed in the house for six days while the bodies were still on the property. It wasn't until January 27 that the grandmother became curious and the police discovered the bodies. By then, the couple had already fled.

The couple then escaped to a farm in Bennet, Nebraska and murdered August Meyer, the owner. They then snagged a ride from two teenagers, Carol King and Robert Jensen, and forced the two to bring them to an abandoned shelter where they were killed. The bodies of Meyer and the teenagers were found in their old car the next day. Next, they targeted the home of C. Lauer Ward, a wealthy industrialist. At that time, his wife, Clara Ward, and their servant, Lillian Fencl, were the only people present. The couple killed Mrs. Ward, and made Lillian prepare breakfast. They killed Mr. Ward when he arrived home in the afternoon, and then tied Lillian to a bed and murdered her too. During this time, the police had begun searching the county for the pair and the FBI was brought in to assist. To divert attention, they dumped their car, and stole a Buick owned by Merle Collison after shooting him to death.

This last car they stole had parking brakes, something Charles wasn't accustomed to. When the car wouldn't move, a passerby offered to help them. Instead, Charles threatened him with a knife. William Romer, the deputy sheriff, was present nearby. He noticed what was happening and called for backup. Caril ran from the car screaming and crying that Charles had killed someone. Charles immediately drove away. The police gave chase and fired shots at the car. The windshield shattered, and Charles began bleeding after he was hit near his ear. He surrendered by pulling over to get medical treatment, because he thought he was mortally wounded.

The couple was arrested. They had their trial in

Nebraska. Initially, Charles said that he forced Caril to go with him, but later he confirmed that she was his accomplice in the murders. Caril kept asserting that she had been taken hostage, but she wasn't believed because she had many chances to get away.

Charles was found to be guilty only for the murder case of Robert Jensen, and was sentenced to death by hanging. Instead, on July 25, 1959, he was executed by electric chair. Caril was sentenced to life imprisonment as his accomplice. She spent seventeen years in the Women's Nebraska Correctional Center in York, and then was released on good behaviour. In 2007, she married a man eleven years older and lived in Michigan, still claiming her innocence. In 2013, she and her husband were in a car accident; her eighty-one-year-old husband died, and she was critically injured.

CHAPTER 17:
CARL "CORAL"
EUGENE WATTS

Knock! Knock! Lenore wasn't expecting anyone, but she went to answer the door. When she opened it, she found a strange black man before her. The man asked for Charles. Before she could tell him that there was no one named Charles there, the man was strangling her. She struggled, and was able to fight him off until he fled. She immediately called the police, but they were unable to make any arrests. Five days later, on October 30, 1974, the same incident happened with Gloria Steele. When she let the stranger in, he attacked her and stabbed her thirty-three times with a knife.

On November 7, 1953, Carl "Coral" Eugene Watts was born to Richard Watts and Dorothy Mae Young. In 1955, his parents got a divorce, and he moved with his mother and younger sister to Inkster, Michigan. Seven years later, his mother remarried. At age eight, he became sick with meningitis, which almost killed him. He suffered from a rising temperature that could have caused minor brain damage. He was forced to miss a year of school because of the illness, and when he came back, his grades declined.

He began to have violent dreams that disturbed his sleeping pattern. He spent his nights fighting off the evil spirit of women and trying to kill them. These weren't nightmares for him really, as he enjoyed them. At age fifteen, he had the urge to act upon these dreams. While delivering newspapers to a woman named Joan Gave, he beat her up and then continued his paper route as if nothing had happened. He was arrested for this incident, and was ordered to go under psychiatric treatment. He finished high school, and went to college on a sports scholarship. However, he came back home after several months to work as a mechanic, and then enrolled at Western Michigan University in Kalamazoo.

His first murder victim was nineteen-year-old Gloria Steele. On November 12, 1974, he attacked another woman in her apartment, but she managed to hold him off and get his license plate number. He was sent to jail for one year for this attack, but never convicted of murder since the prosecutors didn't have any strong evidence against him. When he was released, the series of attacks and murders continued.

On Halloween of 1979, forty-four-year-old Jeanne Clyne, a Detroit News reporter, was walking home from a doctor's appointment when Watts attacked her and stabbed her eleven times. No evidence was found at the scene to lead to a suspect. On April 20, seventeen-year-old Shirley Small was stabbed twice in her heart outside her home at Ann Arbor, Michigan. Later that same summer, a twenty-six-year-old manager of a diner, Glenda Richmond, died of twenty-eight stab wounds to her chest. On September 14, twenty-year-old Rebecca Huff was found dead. Rebecca had been stabbed fifty times. She was the first murder to be linked to Watts, but it took two months before that link was found.

Watts's victims were all females between the ages of fourteen and forty-four. His methods varied; the victims had been strangled, stabbed, bludgeoned, and drowned, usually in their own bathrooms. Between 1974 and 1982, he murdered and attempted to murder dozens of women.

As a result of the constant attacks, police increased patrols in the area of Ann Arbor. They caught a break when two officers arrested Watts after spotting him suspiciously following a woman. They stopped him for driving with expired license plates and a suspended license. When they searched his car, they found a dictionary with the words, "Rebecca is a lover" inside. The dictionary had once belonged to Rebecca Huff.

On August 9, 1982, Watts was offered a deal: if he confessed to the murders, he would be given immunity. He confessed to attacking nineteen women, thirteen of which were murdered. He claimed that his victim count was higher than eighty, but did not give any additional details because he was not given immunity to the murders he may have committed in Michigan and Canada. Watts pled guilty for one count of burglary with intent to kill, as it was in his bargain, and received sixty years in prison. Before leaving, he told one investigator: "*You know, if they ever let me out, I'll kill again.*"

As a "glitch" in the Texas law, he was considered as a nonviolent inmate, and was able to reduce his sentence to be released on May 9, 2006 on good behaviour. Prosecutors did everything possible until they were able to convict him for the murders of Helen Dutcher and Gloria Steele, and he was sentenced for life twice. Watts died in prison of prostate cancer on September 21, 2007.

CHAPTER 18: CHARLES ALBRIGHT

At the 8800 block of Beckleyview, in Dallas, Texas on December 13, 1990, the Oak Cliff neighbourhood kids were hanging out. While there, they stumbled across what seemed to be a mannequin. Upon closer examination, they were shocked to find out that it was a nude body of a dark-haired woman wearing only a bloody t-shirt. She was laying face up covered with blood, with a .44 caliber bullet to the back of her head. Dr. Elizabeth Peacock performed the autopsy. To her surprise, she discovered only muscle and gore under the victim's eyelids. The killer had surgically removed and taken the eyes with him.

Charles Albright was born in Amarillo, Texas on August 10, 1933. He was adopted from an orphanage by Delle and Fred Albright. Delle was a schoolteacher, a strict and overprotective mother who didn't really give Charles the affection he needed. She helped him skip two classes by accelerating his education. He got his first gun as a teenager and started killing small animals. He told his mother that he wanted to become a taxidermist, so she helped him stuff the birds and small animals he killed, but didn't buy him the expensive glass eyes used in taxidermy. Instead, they used buttons.

At the age of thirteen, he was arrested for aggravated assault. He graduated high school when he was fifteen, and lied his way into North Texas University. At sixteen, he was caught with stolen cash, a rifle, and two handguns. He was sent to jail for one year. When he got out, he majored in pre-med studies in Arkansas State Teachers College, but was again found stealing and expelled. He falsified his bachelor's and master's degrees. He married his college girlfriend who was a teacher and had a daughter with her. He couldn't hold a job, but fell into the habit of forging checks. He divorced in 1974. He was again sentenced to two years prison for stealing, but served less than six months. Then, he started gaining the trust of his neighbours. In 1981, after the death of his mother, he was visiting some friends and he sexually molested their daughter who was nine years old. He was prosecuted and received only probation after pleading guilty.

In 1985, he met Dixie (who later became his second wife), invited her to live with him, and soon she began supporting him. He took a paper route early in the morning so he could visit prostitutes without raising Dixie's suspicion.

Three murders were eventually attributed to Charles Albright. The first victim was Mary Lou Pratt (age thirty-three), a prostitute who was found dead on December 13, 1990. Her eyes had been removed. His second victim was another prostitute, Susan Peterson, found on February 10, 1991. She had been dumped in south Dallas, and was shot three times: in the left breast piercing her heart, and in the top and back of her head, entering her brain. She was almost nude, and her t-shirt was pulled up to show her breasts like the previous victim. Again, her eyes were surgically removed. Shirley Williams was the last victim, found naked on March 18, 1991. She was lying on her side near a school, with a broken nose and facial bruises. She was shot on the top of her head and in the face. This time, he was a bit clumsy in removing the eyes, maybe because he was in a rush.

Charles was reported to have been violent with the prostitutes that he picked up, and had also attempted to murder others.

On March 22, 1991, after following many leads, the police arrested Charles Albright in his house. He was charged with one murder, that of Shirley Williams, but prosecutors tried to connect it to the other murders. The prosecution was able to link a hair found on the victim to Albright. However, the case still seemed circumstantial. On December 18, 1991, the jury found Charles guilty of the murder of Williams only. At eighty-one years old, he currently is imprisoned in Clements Unit in Amarillo, Texas and is still fascinated with eyes.

CHAPTER 19: CHARLES CULLEN

Something was shady about Nurse Charles. He cared for the patients and completed his shifts, but still a lot of patients in the various hospitals he worked for suffered from a sudden weird death. However, his records showed nothing.

Charles Edmond Cullen was born in West Orange, New Jersey, on February 22, 1960. He was the youngest of eight children. His father died at the age of fifty-eight, when Charles was just seven months old. Cullen's childhood was miserable, and he often attempted suicide. His first attempt to kill himself was when he was nine, by drinking chemicals from a chemistry set. On December 6, 1977, his mother died in a car accident in which his sister was driving; this left him devastated. In April 1978, Cullen dropped out of high school. He then enlisted in the U.S. Navy. He rose in ranks until he started to exhibit signs of mental instability. He tried to commit suicide several more times until he was discharged from the Navy for medical reasons on March 30, 1984. He later began working as a nurse in various hospitals.

Charles Cullen's first murder is unknown. On June 11, 1988, Judge John W. Yengo was admitted to St.

Barnabas Medical Center suffering from a severe allergic reaction to a blood-thinning drug. During his hospital stay, Charles gave him an overdose of intravenous medication to kill him. At that hospital, he also killed several patients, including an AIDS patient to whom he gave an insulin overdose. He quit his job there after an investigation began looking into the contamination of the IV bags with insulin. Cullen was responsible for dozens of deaths this way, but he wasn't suspected of any wrongdoings.

In February 1992, Cullen started working at Warren Hospital in Phillipsburg, New Jersey. There, three elderly women were killed by an overdose of digoxin, a heart medication. In December 1993, he quit, and began working in the intensive care and cardiac care unit in Hunterdon Medical Center in Flemington, New Jersey. According to Cullen, he killed five patients there between January and September 1996 with overdoses of digoxin. After that, he found work at Morristown Memorial Hospital, but was fired for poor performance in August 1997. Two months later, he was admitted to a psychiatric facility to treat his depression, but left after a short time. His mental health stayed poor.

In February 1998, he got a job in the Liberty Nursing and Rehabilitation Center in Allentown, Pennsylvania. There he worked in the ward of respirator-dependent patients. During that time, another nurse was fired for a patient's death that Cullen murdered. In October 1998, Cullen again was fired after he was seen entering a patient's room with a syringe; the patient lived but ended up with a broken arm. The hospital didn't report any deaths, and Cullen's record still showed nothing. From November 1998 to March 1999, Cullen worked at Easton Hospital in Easton, Pennsylvania, where he killed another patient with digoxin. There was an internal investigation within the hospital, but it was inconclusive. Again, Cullen got away with murder. He continued his murders and periodic suicide attempts until 2003. The speculation surrounding him was on the rise, especially with his many odd drug requests.

He was eventually hired at New Jersey's Somerset Medical Center. There, he killed thirteen patients over thirteen months by lethal injections. However, it wasn't until Roman Catholic priest Reverend Florian Gall died by digoxin injections while recovering from pneumonia that an investigation was opened.

Charles Cullen was arrested on December 12, 2003, and was charged with one count of murder and one count of attempted murder. In 2004, he pleaded guilty to thirteen murders in New Jersey. He was cooperative with law enforcement and identified many of his victims. He confessed to killing forty patients that he could recall during his sixteen-year career as a nurse, but his victims are estimated to have been in the hundreds. He didn't have memories of murdering all his victims.

He was tried on March 10, 2006, and sentenced to 127 years in prison. He claimed his motive was that he wanted to end the suffering of the patients, although some of them weren't actually dying.

CHAPTER 20: CHARLES NG

The man told the officer, who was arresting him for owning an illegal weapon, that he had not thought an awful bench vise could bring him to this. He continued by saying that the name of his friend was Charles Chi-Tat Ng (pronounced Cheetah Ing). Then he revealed that Leonard Lake was his actual name and he was a wanted criminal by the FBI. He then slipped two cyanide capsules into his mouth and went into spasms. He was barely alive when taken to the hospital and died a few days later. The search for the so-called Charles began.

Charles Chi-Tat Ng was born in Hong Kong on December 24, 1960. His father was a wealthy Chinese executive who abused and disciplined him. Charles started stealing at an early age, was arrested at age fifteen for shoplifting, and was rusticated from a boarding school of Lancashire, England, also for stealing. Then, he travelled to the U.S. on a student Visa, and received admission in the Notre Dame de Namur University of California, but dropped out after one semester. Soon after, he was involved in a hit and run accident, and signed up for the U.S. Marine Corps to avoid prosecution. Around that time, he met Leonard Lake.

After serving in the Marine Corps for less than one year, Charles was discharged for theft, but escaped being court-martialed by running away and therefore avoided imprisonment. He was later captured and sentenced to fourteen years in a military prison, but was released in 1982. After his release, he contacted Leonard Lake immediately.

Lake invited Charles Ng to his place. It was a remote cabin near Wilseyville, California. A dungeon was built near the cabin, where abductions, rapes, tortures, and killings would take place over the next year.

The two men lured eighteen-year-old Kathleen Allen to the cabin by telling her that her boyfriend, Michael Sean Carroll (Charles's previous cellmate in prison) had been shot. They forced her to perform a striptease while taunting her and filming the whole thing, then Charles was seen cavorting on a bed with Kathleen until later they murdered her. Her boyfriend had already been killed at this point.

Their nineteen-year-old neighbour, Brenda O'Connor, was also lured to the house. After killing her common-law husband Lonnie Bond and their baby Lonnie Jr., they taped, tortured, raped, and killed her.

Their other victims included Robin Scott Stapley, Randy Johnson, Paul Cosner, Harvey Dubs, Deborah Dubs, and their son Sean Dubs. Before each murder, they filmed themselves while torturing and raping the female victims. In the end, it is believed that the two men murdered and buried between eleven and twenty-five victims at Lake's ranch.

Charles Ng was also addicted to stealing. On June 2, 1985, the vise they were using to torture their victims broke, so Lake and Ng were looking to replace it.

Charles tried to shoplift a new vise from a hardware shop when the police were called. Charles left on foot and disappeared, but Leonard was arrested and he swallowed the cyanide pills.

The investigation led the police to the dungeon near the cabin, where they found burned and smashed human bones and a map that led them to envelopes containing victim IDs, journals that Lake wrote in 1983 and 1984, and videotapes of them torturing two of their victims.

Charles escaped to Calgary, Alberta, but police arrested him on June 6, 1985 for a robbery at The Bay departmental store. He was charged with attempted robbery, robbery, attempted murder, and custody of a firearm. He was convicted and sentenced to four and a half years in a Canadian prison. Charles was later extradited to California after a legal battle. There he was prosecuted and tried for twelve counts of murder in 1998. His trial took eight months. On February 24, 1999, the jury found him guilty for the murder of three women, two male infants, and six men, and sentenced him to death. Currently, Charles Ng is on Death Row at the San Quentin State Prison.

CHAPTER 21: CHARLES PANZRAM

aka Carl Panzram

Charles Panzram was a person who was full of hate and did not have room for feelings like honour, decency, pity, love, or kindness. His only regret was that he was not born dead! In 1928, he was arrested for burglary in Washington, D.C. While he was being interrogated for the burglary, he voluntarily confessed to an awful crime: murder. His "out of the blue" confession included the murder of two boys.

Charles (also known as Carl) Panzram was born on July 28, 1891, to Johann "John" and Matilda Panzram, two Prussian immigrants, in East Grand Forks, Minnesota. When he was twelve, his parents sent him to the Minnesota State Training School. The staff members there repeatedly raped, beat, and tortured him. Two years later, he was released from the school. Entering his teen years, he became an alcoholic, a burglar, and a thief. He ran away from home when he was fourteen, and he claimed that he had been gang raped by a group of hobos.

Before the year 1920, he was involved in many thefts and was imprisoned various times. On June 1, 1915, after burglarizing a house in Astoria, Oregon, he was arrested and sentenced to seven years in prison. In 1917, he helped his inmate Otto Hooker escape from the prison. Hooker killed the warden, Harry Minto, during his escape. This was Panzram's first contact with murder. He was caught and brought back to prison, but he escaped again on May 2, 1918. Leaving prison behind, he headed east, changed his name, and shaved off his moustache.

In the summer of 1920, he burglarized the home of William H. Taft (the then Secretary of War and future U.S. President). He stole several valuables and a .45 Colt handgun, which he later used in many murders. He bought a yacht and began cruising along the East River. He raped and killed the sailors he hired as crew and threw their bodies in the ocean. In August, a storm caused him to lose the boat.

He moved to Lobito Bay, where he hired six locals to help him in his crocodile hunting expedition. When the crocodiles appeared, he shot the locals and fed their bodies to the reptiles. After that, he fled to the Gold Coast, the Canary Islands, Lisbon in Portugal, and then back to America in the summer of 1922, where he raped and killed two boys in addition to committing robbery and arson. He was imprisoned again in 1923, and was often abused and tortured. During that prison stay, he was moved by an act of kindness made by a young guard, Henry Lesser, who sent him a dollar to buy cigarettes and extra food. Henry also provided him with writing materials so he could write his autobiography, where he described his crimes in detail, as well as how he had been tortured in jail. He wrote: "In my lifetime, I murdered 21 human beings, I committed thousands of burglaries, robberies, larcenies, arsons, and last but not least I have committed sodomy on more than 1,000 male human beings." The most astonishing factor is that he wasn't sorry for what he had done!

After his arrest, he confessed to the murder of twenty-one victims, all of which he raped and tortured before killing. He also admitted to the thousands of sodomy acts he performed on his victims. His only motive: hate. He raped his victims to humiliate them. He acted as his own defense in his trial, and was found guilty and sentenced to twenty-five years in Fort Leavenworth. When he arrived, he told the warden, "I'll kill the first man that bothers me." He kept his promise when he attacked his supervisor with a heavy iron bar and bludgeoned him to death on June 20, 1929. Again, he acted as his own defense in his trial on April 14, 1930. He was found guilty and seemed happy to have been sentenced to death by hanging. He refused any attempts made by groups advocating the abolishing of the death penalty to reduce his sentence.

When asked if he had any last words by the executioner, he said: "Yes, hurry it up, you Hoosier bastard! I could kill 10 men while you're fooling around!" On September 5, 1930, he was hanged and pronounced dead at 6:18 a.m. He was buried in the prison cemetery.

CHAPTER 22:
CHARLES RAY
HATCHER

In the spring of 1935, Charles and his older brother Arthur found a copper wire in an old Ford Model T, so they decided to make a kite, and fly it. The kite was with Arthur but it was Charles's turn to fly it. Arthur was about to give the kite to his brother, when suddenly it hit a high-voltage power line and Charles watched him get electrocuted. Arthur was pronounced dead at the scene. This horrible incident traumatized little Charles for life.

Charles Ray Hatcher was born on July 16, 1929, the youngest of four children of Jesse and Lula Hatcher. His father was an abusive alcoholic and an ex-convict as well. After the incident that led to the death of his older brother, his parents got a divorce. His mother remarried, and he moved with her and his stepfather to St. Joseph in 1945.

His criminal life began in his early teen years. Between ages eighteen and thirty-four, he was in and out of prison numerous times, mostly for robbery and assault. His killings began in 1961, while in prison.

On July 2, 1961, Charles raped and killed fellow inmate Jerry Tharrington, but there was no evidence to convict him. Instead, he was sent to solitary for a month. On August 24, 1963, he was released from prison for good behaviour.

On August 27, 1969, in Antioch, California, he lured twelve-year-old William Freeman to a creek and strangled him. Two days later, he offered six-year-old Gilbert Martinez ice cream. Later, the boy was found dead after being beaten and sexually assaulted. Charles was using the alias Albert Ralph Price at the time, and was ultimately charged with assault, sodomy, and kidnapping attempts. In 1970, he was bouncing back and forth between courts and was ordered to undergo psychological evaluations by several psychiatrists. During his evaluations, he tried to exaggerate his mental disorders. On May 24, 1971, he was sent to trial and pleaded not guilty by reason of insanity. In August 1972, he was seen fit to stand trial. In December, he was convicted for the abduction and molestation of Martinez, and committed to the California State Hospital as a mentally disordered sexual offender. He attempted to escape but was unsuccessful. On May 20, 1977, he was released to a halfway house in San Francisco, but he just couldn't stay out of trouble.

On May 26, 1978, four-year-old Eric Christgen disappeared in downtown Saint Joseph, Missouri. He was sexually abused and then suffocated. A twenty-five-year-old man named Melvin Reynolds was questioned in the disappearance and taken into custody. He was wrongfully convicted of second-degree murder, and was sentenced to life imprisonment. Investigators wouldn't learn until later that Charles was the real killer. Melvin was released when Charles confessed.

On September 4, 1978, he was arrested under the pseudonym of Richard Clark for sexually assaulting a sixteen-year-old boy in Nebraska. He was released in January 1979 for the assault of Thomas Morton (age seven), and was sent to a mental hospital, but the charges were dropped. In 1980, he was arrested for the attempted assault and sodomy of a seventeen-year-old boy. I don't understand why he kept getting released. With his record, there was no doubt he would re-offend. How many victims could have been saved?

Eleven-year-old Michelle Steele was later found beaten and strangled to death near St Joseph, on the Missouri River. Charles was arrested the next day. While he was waiting for the trial, he confessed to the murder of fifteen children since 1969. He confessed to the murders of William Freeman (age twelve) and Eric Christgen. He also led the investigators to the remains of James Churchill. In October 1983, he was convicted of the murder of Eric, and was sentenced to life imprisonment without parole for at least fifty years. A year later, he was also convicted for the murder of Michelle Steele, and was again sentenced to life imprisonment in 1984. In December of that year, Charles hanged himself in his cell at the Missouri State Penitentiary in Jefferson City.

CHAPTER 23: CHARLES STARKWEATHER

On November 30, 1957, Charles Starkweather tried to buy a stuffed animal at the Lincoln service station. Robert Colvert, the station's attendant, refused to give him the animal on credit. Charles became angry and left. Later that night, he returned several times to make small purchases, until finally he waved his gun at Robert, forced him to give him $100, drove him to a remote area, and shot him.

Charles Starkweather was born on November 24, 1938. His parents were Guy, a carpenter, and Helen, a waitress. His family was respected within the community because of their well-mannered children, but they were still poor. Charles attended the Saratoga Elementary School, Everett Junior High School, and Lincoln High School. He was born with a minor birth defect, Genu Varum, also known as "bowleggedness." He had also suffered from a speech disorder that made him a target for bullying, and a severe myopia, which held him back in school. He excelled in gym class, where he found an outlet for all his rage and anger towards those who bullied him, until he started bullying his bullies and anyone else back. After watching James Dean's movie "Rebel without a Cause," Charles related to Dean's defiant screen persona. He was rusticated from high school in his senior year. In 1956, he was introduced through a friend to Caril Ann Fugate who was five years younger than he, and they began dating.

His first murder was of Robert Colvert in 1957. He confessed to his girlfriend about the robbery, but claimed that someone else had killed him. She didn't believe him. On January 21, 1958, Charles went to Caril's home to see her, but she wasn't there. When Caril's stepfather and mother told him to stay away, he shot them, and then strangled and stabbed their baby, Betty Jean (age two). When Caril arrived home, she helped him hide the bodies. The two remained in the house for six days, until Caril's suspicious grandmother alerted the police. The couple then went on a killing spree.

They drove to a farmhouse in Bennet, Nebraska, where Charles shot August Meyer (age seventeen) in the head, and killed his dog. They abandoned their car, and were offered a ride by two teenagers, Carol King and Robert Jensen. Charles forced both to drive to a forsaken storm shelter where he killed Robert. He tried to rape Carol but was unable to perform, which made him angry so he shot her. Caril was jealous, so she mutilated Carol's genitals. Then the couple escaped using Robert's car. They moved to a populated and wealthy part of Lincoln. There, they broke into the home of C. Lauer Ward, an industrialist, and they killed Clara, his wife, by stabbing her. They then forced the servant, Lillian

Fencl, to make them breakfast and they then stabbed her as well. When Mr. Ward came back home, Charles shot him. They stole jewelry and took Ward's black 1956 Packard, and escaped from Nebraska. This murder prompted law enforcement to widen the investigation for the murderers.

Charles and Caril needed to dump the Packard in order to keep a low profile, so they found a Buick to steal. Merle Collison, a traveling salesman, was sleeping in the Buick, so the couple woke him up, shot him, and stole the car.

The Buick had a parking brake, something that Charles wasn't accustomed to, and the car wouldn't move. A passer-by stopped to try and help, and instead Charles threatened the person with his rifle. A nearby deputy sheriff noticed the altercation and called for back up. Just then, Caril ran to the officer screaming that Charles was trying to kill her. Charles then returned to the Packard and tried to evade the police. The police fired, and a bullet shattered the windshield, injuring Charles. Believing he was fatally injured, he surrendered to receive medical care.

Charles was extradited to Nebraska, and tried there. First, he claimed that he had forced Caril to be with him, but then testified that she was an enthusiastic participant. He received the death penalty for murdering Robert Jensen. On June 25, 1959, he was put to death by electric chair.

CHAPTER 24: CHRISTOPHER BERNARD WILDER

The story of Christopher Wilder is the story of someone who had been close to death so many times that his life had escalated to being a death bringer.

On March 13, 1945, Christopher Bernard Wilder was born in Sydney, Australia. His father was an American naval officer, and his mother a native Australian. Immediately after his birth, he came so close to dying that a priest performed Last Rites, but he recovered. When he was two years old, he almost drowned in a swimming pool. The next year, he fainted from a fit of convulsions.

His life took a wild turn in his teen years. In his early adolescence, he started peeking through windows. At seventeen, he was arrested with his friends for the gang rape of a girl on a Sydney beach. He pleaded guilty and received one year of probation along with electroshock therapy. At twenty-three, he got married, but his wife left him eight days later, after she discovered his dark sexual tendencies. In 1969, Wilder immigrated to the U.S. and settled in Florida. There, he led a successful and rich life.

Beginning in 1971, he was arrested many times for sexual offenses. Once he lured a schoolgirl out of a shopping mall, drugged her, and then forced her to have sex with him in his truck. He was charged but managed to plea-bargain the charges. He visited a sex therapist who believed that Wilder was making progress throughout their sessions. However, when he was visiting his parents in Australia, he kidnapped two teenage girls, tied them up, forced them to pose nude for pictures, masturbated over them, and then he released them. The girls went to the police, and he was arrested but his parents bailed him out. He was allowed to return to Florida until his trial, which kept being postponed until he managed to escape.

Wilder's first known murder victim was Rosario Gonzalez, who was last seen on February 26, 1984, at the Miami Grand Prix. On March 4, 1984, twenty-three-year-old Elizabeth Kenyon, who was Wilder's ex-girlfriend, went missing. Wilder quickly became a suspect. The police found a link between the disappearance of Gonzalez and Kenyon, and everything was leading to Wilder. Before he could be arrested, he fled and his killing spree started.

The day after fleeing, Wilder picked up Terry Ferguson (age twenty-one) from a shopping mall in Florida, and he killed her. Then he left her body in a snake-infested canal. It wasn't found until five days later. His next target was Linda Grover (age nineteen) whom he also took from a shopping mall to a motel in Bainbridge, Georgia. There he raped her twice and electrocuted her. However, she was able to run to the bathroom and cried for help. Wilder panicked and escaped.

In Beaumont, Texas, he tried to lure twenty-four-year-old Terry Walden someplace where he promised to take her photographs, but she denied him. Two days later, Walden disappeared, and her body was found with stab wound three days later. The FBI was called in to help with the case.

On March 25, Suzanne Logan (age twenty-one) went missing from an Oklahoma shopping mall. She was found dead the next day. Eighteen-year-old Sheryl Bonaventura also disappeared from a Colorado shopping mall. He kept her hostage until March 31, when he killed her. The next day, Michelle Korfman (age seventeen) disappeared. Wilder landed himself a spot on the FBI's Ten Most Wanted list by this time. Soon after, he kidnapped Marie Risico (age sixteen) and assaulted her. He didn't kill her, but forced her to help him abduct more victims. He drove her to Gary, Indiana, and forced her to lure sixteen-year-old Dawnete Wilt into the car. He attacked Wilt and raped her in the car while Risico drove. He kept threatening to kill both girls if they tried to escape. He continued torturing Wilt by electrocution and rape. The next day, he took them to a forest in New York, and stabbed Wilt in the front and back, leaving her for dead, but she survived. Beth Dodge (age thirty-three) was another victim. He then released Risico who returned home and went to the local police.

Wilder continued his killing spree without much of a cooling off period, until he got near the Canadian border where two state troopers recognized him. When they approached him, he reached for his revolver, and fired two shots: one shot went wild and the other wounded one of the state troopers who returned fire. One of the bullets hit Wilder in the heart and killed him. This ended his twenty-six days of killing.

CHAPTER 25: CLIFFORD OLSON

On the evening of June 21, 1981, Jim Parranto was driving though Weaver Lake. Suddenly, he saw a man next to a pickup truck, bending over a body. The body was a young girl, later identified as Ada Court. Jim pulled off the road to help the man, assuming that he was in trouble. When Jim asked the man if he needed any help, the man turned and just stared at him. Jim got out of there, but it wasn't until a few months later that he reported the incident.

Clifford Robert Olson, Jr. was born on January 1, 1940, a New Year's baby. His parents were an ordinary couple, and Clifford had two other younger brothers and a sister. When Clifford was five, they returned to the West Coast. As a child, Clifford would do anything to be the centre of attention. He didn't really have any close friends, and even in his early years, he would capture and torture animals.

In 1956, he left high school. In July of the next year, he was sentenced to a correctional centre for breaking and entering, as well as theft. He spent most of his life in prison for various charges, such as possession of stolen property and firearms, fraud, obstructing justice, false pretenses, theft, breaking and entering, parole violation, armed robbery, impaired driving, and escape from custody. In just twenty-four years, he had eighty-three convictions. By the time he was forty-one years old, he had spent just four years of freedom outside the prison in his adult life. Prison had become his home. His fellow inmates hated him because he was an informant and a snitch.

Clifford's first murder victim was twelve-year-old Christine Weller. She was stabbed to death in the abdomen and chest, and strangled with a belt on November 16, 1980. A few months later, on April 16, 1981, thirteen-year-old Colleen Marian Daignault disappeared. Her skeletal remains wouldn't be found until September 17. On April 22, 1981, sixteen-year-old Daryn Johnsrude also disappeared. She was bludgeoned to death, and her body wouldn't be found until May 2. On June 21, 1981, thirteen-year-old Ada Anita Court disappeared. Clifford was a prime suspect in the disappearance of Ada. Initially, the young girls were considered to be runaways, and not murder victims. It wasn't until the disappearance of nine-year-old Simon Partington on July 2, 1981 that the police began considering a serial killer might be responsible for the murders. Simon couldn't be considered as a runaway, as he was too young.

The series of murders in 1981 continued. On July 9, Judy Kozma (age fifteen) was raped and then strangled. She was found dead on July 25. Raymond King Jr. (age fifteen) was kidnapped on July 23. He was raped and bludgeoned. A German tourist, Sirgun Arnd (age eighteen), was raped and bludgeoned on July 25. She also couldn't be considered as a runaway. Two days later, Terri Lyn Carson (age fifteen) was raped and strangled. On July 30, Louise Chartrand (age seventeen) was also murdered.

The case was confusing and difficult for police to piece together, since Clifford chose both male and female victims of various ages. He also tried to copy another rapist murderer, Gary Francis Marcoux, whom he had met while serving time.

On August 12, 1981, Clifford was arrested for attempting to kidnap two girls. On August 25, he was charged with the murder of Judy Kozma. He then struck a deal with the authorities: he would confess to eleven murders and lead them to where some of the undiscovered bodies were buried, and in exchange, the authorities would pay $10,000 for each victim to Clifford's wife who collected $100,000 (the information on the eleventh murder was free). In January of 1982, Clifford pleaded guilty to the murders. He received the highest count of life sentences that could be received in Canada.   He served his sentence in a maximum-security prison. On September 30, 2011, Clifford died from cancer at the age of seventy-one.

CHAPTER 26:
COLIN IRELAND

The Coleherne is a gay pub in west London. The men who frequent this pub are often looking for sexual partners, and they wear colour-coded handkerchiefs to indicate which role they prefer: top or bottom. A man named Colin frequented this bar, and sought men who wore the colour indicating that they would take the passive role. However, he chose his victims for much more than an innocent sexual game.

Colin Ireland's parents were teenagers when his seventeen-year-old mother became pregnant. He was born on March 16, 1954, in Dartford, Kent. Shortly after his birth, his father deserted them. They lived with his mother's parents for some years, and then moved out. She couldn't really support them, and they lived a poor life. His mother eventually married an electrician, Saker Ireland, who gave Colin his last name. The marriage didn't last long. They got divorced and were always on the move, which made it difficult for Colin to adjust. During his teen years, he was approached many times by older men offering him something in exchange for sexual services. He never accepted, but this situation fueled his anger and rage.

Colin was highly organized in his murders, carrying a full murder kit with him for his crimes. He was not sexually motivated; instead, he killed others out of hatred and with a desire to be somebody. He was very careful not leave anything at the crime scene that would link him to the murders. He would even stay in the flat where he killed his victims until morning so he wouldn't raise suspicion, and he would clean everything to remove any forensic evidence. He was a psychopath.

His first victim was forty-five-year-old Peter Walker, who liked sadomasochism. He took Colin to his flat where Colin suffocated him with a plastic bag, and placed two teddy bears in a 69 position on the body. The next day, when he didn't hear any news about the murder, he informed the Samaritans (a charity for the emotionally distressed) and a journalist from *The Sun* newspaper about the murder.

His next victim was thirty-seven-year-old Christopher Dunn, who was a librarian. He was found naked in a harness. At first, his death wasn't linked to Walker's because they lived in a different area, and different investigators were working on the cases.

Colin's third victim was thirty-five-year-old Perry Bradly III. At first, Perry didn't like the idea of getting tied up, but Colin persuaded him. Suddenly, Perry found himself with a noose around his neck on his bed. Colin then threatened that he would torture him and demanded Perry's money and ATM pin number, assuring him that he was just a thief. After getting the information, Colin told Perry he would leave him unharmed and that he should go to sleep. Knowing that Perry could identify him, Colin strangled him with the noose, and placed a doll on top of the dead body.

Colin was angry that there was no publicity after these murders, so the next day he killed thirty-three-year-old Andrew Collier after killing his cat and demanding his ATM pin number. He strangled him with a noose, put a condom on his penis, and put the cat's mouth on it. He then put a condom on the cat's tail and placed that into Andrew's mouth, in order to create a link with Walker's murder. Unfortunately for him, he left some fingerprints in the flat.

His last murder was of forty-one-year-old Emanuel Spiteri. He again demanded the victim to give him his ATM pin number, and killed him with a noose. He cleaned any evidence and set the place on fire. He called the police informing them of the murder, and said that he probably wouldn't kill again.

The police eventually connected the five murders. The investigation uncovered that Colin had been seen with his last victim. Colin claimed that he had been with Spiteri, but did not kill him. However, his fingerprints connected him to Collier's murder.

He was charged with the murders of Collier and Spiteri, and confessed to the other three. He pleaded guilty in his 1993 trial, and was given five sentences of life imprisonment. He was called "The Gay Slayer." On February 21, 2012, he died in prison from pulmonary fibrosis and a fractured hip.

CHAPTER 27: DAVID BERKOWITZ

aka Son of Sam

"He told me to kill. Sam is the devil." These words were spoken by David Berkowitz when he was questioned for murder. He explained that his fellow citizen Sam Carr supervised him for the murder by sending messages through his dog.

David Berkowitz was born Richard David Falco on June 1, 1953. A few days later, he was adopted by Pearl and Nathan Berkowitz. He was a troubled child while growing up, but showed signs of extraordinary intelligence. When he was still a teen, his mother died. He was largely affected by her death, since he was close to her and used to share his important moments with her.

When he was eighteen, he joined the U.S. Army. In 1974, he was honourably discharged. He then successfully located his real mother Betty Falco. She told him all about his illicit birth, something that disturbed him, especially when he learned that his father was dead. He lost contact with his real mother, but stayed in contact with his half-sister. His neighbours and his co-workers described him as a loner.

David's first murder was on December 24, 1975. He stabbed two women with a knife, killing one (who was never identified), and seriously injuring the other (Michelle Forman), which put her in the hospital.

David's killing spree began on July 29, 1976. Outside the Bronx apartment building, he killed two young girls, Donna Lauria (age eighteen) and Jody Valenti (age nineteen), who were sitting in a car. Lauria was killed instantly, and Valenti was injured. His next murder happened within three months. Carl Denaro (age twenty-five) and Rosemary Keenan (age twenty-eight) were sitting in a parked car when they were shot by David; Carl's skull was severely damaged and Rosemary was injured. On November of the same year, he shot two teenage girls, Donna DeMasi (age sixteen) and Joanne Lomino (age eighteen), who were walking home; Lomino was left paraplegic, but they both survived.

On January 30, 1977, engaged couple John Diel (age thirty) and Christine Freund (age twenty-six) were shot while sitting in their car. John drove away immediately and suffered from minor injuries, but Christine was shot twice and died several hours later that night. The police now realized that they might have a serial killer, since all the shootings seemed similar. On March 8, Virginia Voskerichian (age nineteen), was walking home from her college classes. She attempted to defend herself but was shot in the head and killed instantly.

On April 17, another couple, Alexander Esau (age twenty) and Valentina Suriani (age eighteen), was shot in their car in the Bronx. Valentina died immediately, while Alexander died a few hours later. At this scene, a handwritten letter was left for the NYPD's Captain

Joseph Borrelli. In this letter, David Berkowitz called himself the "Son of Sam." For all the murders, a .44 Caliber was used.

Another attack struck another young couple, Sal Lupo (age twenty) and Judy Placido (age seventeen), on June 26. Both were shot in their car, but they survived. The last murder was on July 31, 1977. Bobby Violante and Stacy Moskowitz (both age twenty) were shot. Stacy died, and Bobby lost one eye due to the injuries and lost most of his vision in the other eye. However, this time a witness had seen something that helped crack the case.

At the spot of the final murder, a local resident named Cecilia Davis saw a man rushing away in a car with a parking ticket on it. Luckily, only a handful of parking tickets had been handed that day, and one of them was for David Berkowitz. On August 10, 1977, Berkowitz was arrested. Months were spent to determine if he was fit to stand for trial. After many psychological examinations, he confessed the six murders in August 1978. He was sentenced to twenty-five years of life imprisonment for each murder.

Currently, David Berkowitz is serving time at the Sullivan Correctional Facility in Fallsburg, New York. In prison, he became a devout Christian. He asked that his 2012 hearing be cancelled, stating he deserved to spend the rest of his life in prison.

CHAPTER 28:
DAVID CARPENTER

August 19, 1979 was a nice day for a hike in Marin County, California. Edda Kane, a forty-four-year-old married bank executive, liked to keep an athletic lifestyle. She wanted to hike the trails in a park at the foot of Mount Tamalpais, but found no one to go with her, so she decided to go alone. She never returned.

David Joseph Carpenter was born on May 6, 1930, in San Francisco, California. He was abused by his alcoholic father and domineering mother. At age seven, he began stuttering, making it difficult for him to make friends, which would lead to him being constantly teased. He also had a bed-wetting problem, and he began torturing animals. At age seventeen, he was sent to jail for molesting his two younger cousins, but was released a year later.

He continued molesting children until 1955, when he got married and later became the father of three children. He worked in different jobs and even rendered his services to the Coast Guard. He continued to stalk women, and in 1960, he lured a woman into the woods of Presidio, tied her up with clothesline, injured her with his hammer, and wounded her hand. Luckily, a military patrol official who happened to be in the area saved the woman, and David was arrested. He was sentenced to fourteen years of prison for one count of stabbing with intention to kill and two counts of beating with a dangerous weapon. Later, his wife divorced him. He was released from jail after serving nine years of his sentence. He continued his series of attacks against women, and between January 27 and February 3, he attacked, raped, or tried to rape four women. He was arrested again, and was charged for kidnapping and robbery. In May 1979, he was released on a conditional period to the federal halfway house.

Carpenter's first murder was of Edda Kane on that August day in 1979. It looked as though she had been attacked from behind. She was shot in the back of her head. The position of her knees and face on the ground showed that she had been forced to beg for her life. The killer took $10 from her wallet, some credit cards, and her glasses, but left her jewelry.

On October 21, another victim met her fate at the hands of David Carpenter. Twenty-three-year-old Mary Frances Bennett was stabbed to death. He waited until March 1980 to strike again. Twenty-three-year-old Barbara Schwartz was out hiking with her dog when David encountered her and stabbed her to death in the chest. A passerby saw the scene, led the rangers to the crime scene, and gave them a description of the murderer that misled the investigation for a while. David wasn't suspected because he didn't seem to fit the description.

On October 11, Richard "Rick" Stowers (age nineteen) and Cindy Moreland (age eighteen) were shot in the head and killed. On October 15, Anne Alderson (age twenty-six) went jogging in woods, but was raped and shot in the head with a .38 caliber gun. Another victim was claimed in late November, Shauna May. He raped her, bound her with a wire, shot her three times, and left her body near the dead body of another victim, Diana O'Connell (age twenty-two). His last victim was Heather Scaggs (age twenty). This time, she wasn't killed on a hiking trail like the others; instead, David lured her away by offering to sell a used car. Heather was raped and shot through the eye also with a .38, and her body wasn't found until weeks later.

The FBI had become involved at this point. The investigators were interested in David Carpenter because he was connected to one of the victims and he had prior sex offenses. David was arrested, and the investigators examined his car. There, they found guides to nearby hiking trails and the .38 revolver used in the murders. In addition, many witnesses saw David and his car at the places of the attacks. However, due to the lack of forensic evidence, he was only charged and tried for the murders of Cindy Moreland, Rick Stowers, Anne Alderson, and Shauna May. He was found guilty of first-degree murder and sentenced to death by the gas chamber. In the year 2009, the San Francisco police used DNA evidence to connect Carpenter to the death of Mary Frances Bennett. To this day, he is still waiting on Death Row for his life to come to an end.

CHAPTER 29: DAYTON LEROY ROGERS

Everett Banyard, a crossbow hunter, was pursuing prey in a private farm southeast of Molalla, Oregon. It was a nice day on August 31, 1987. Suddenly, Everett saw something unfamiliar. He got closer to investigate. That was when he stumbled upon a gruesome discovery: a nude body of a young woman partly covered by the brush. As quickly as possible, Everett reported what he found to the authorities.

Dayton Leroy Rogers was born in Idaho on September 30, 1953. His parents moved around a lot. Along the way, they adopted four more children, and Rogers lost his place as the only child of the family. His criminal life began at a young age. When he was just sixteen, he and a friend began shooting bullets at passing cars, attempting to break a windshield. This was just the beginning.

On August 25, 1972, he drove his fifteen-year-old girlfriend to the woods, stabbed her in the stomach with a hunting knife, and then drove her to the hospital. In February 1973, he received a sentence of four years of probation. Nearly one year after his first attack, on August 1, 1973, he attacked two fifteen-year-old girls with a beer bottle. He was charged of second- and third-degree assault, but was committed to a state hospital for mental illness. He was released on December 12, 1974. On February 24, 1976, he raped a high school girl, and threatened another with a knife. He continued this process of getting sentenced and released until August 1987.

In the very early morning of August 7, 1987, Dayton Rogers was found in a Portland parking lot. He was crouching over a nude, mutilated body. A few minutes earlier, the woman had been screaming, "Please help me! Rape! I'm being raped!" Since it was still pre-dawn, only a few people heard her and ran to help. As they came closer, the horrible picture became clearer. As the crowd gathered, the man, Rogers, had headed toward a small foreign pickup parked nearby. Two bystanders rushed over to see what had happened, and after seeing the woman, they attempted to block Rogers from getting away. But he drove around them, out over the sidewalk. One of the men was determined to catch him, so he chased in pursuit after the pickup, at speeds of over 100 miles per hour. The man got close enough to get the license plate of the pickup, and then gave up the chase. When he got back, he gave this information to the police. It turned out that the woman was Jennifer Lisa Smith, a convicted prostitute and drug addict. She had been stabbed eleven times. She was moved to the hospital, but pronounced dead on arrival.

Due to the license plate information, and the many witnesses that night, Rogers was arrested at home. When searching his truck, the police found bloodstains and fingerprints that matched Smith, his last victim. Many witnesses identified Rogers as the attacker.

On August 31, 1987, Banyard found the nude body of a woman decomposing in a private farm near Molalla. By sundown on September 1, the remains of four other victims were also discovered nearby. By September 5, seven bodies had been discovered in all. Each victim had been fatally stabbed after torture and mutilation. The victims were later identified as twenty-three-year-old Lisa Mock, a prostitute and an addict, twenty-six-year-old Maureen Hodges, a junkie, thirty-five-year-old Christine Adams, twenty-six-year-old Nondace Cervantes, sixteen-year-old Reatha Gayles, a high school student, twenty-one-year-old Cynthia DeVore, and one unidentified body.

Rogers was the prime suspect in all these murders. Linking all the victims together was that the fact that most of them were prostitutes, Rogers' type, and at the crime scene, miniature vodka bottles and disposable orange juice bottles were found, the same kind that was in the back of Rogers' pickup. However, there wasn't enough forensic evidence to indict him, so he was only charged with the murder of Jennifer Lisa Smith. He was tried in January 1988, but claimed he killed her in self-defense. Still, he was found guilty of aggravated murder on February 20, and was sentenced to life imprisonment, with a minimum of thirty years before any parole.

CHAPTER 30: DENNIS NILSEN

The story of Dennis Nilsen is proof enough that a lonely heart is a dangerous one.

Dennis Andrew Nilsen was born on November 23, 1945. His father was alcoholic. His parents' marriage wasn't a happy one and they divorced when he was four years old. He moved with his mother and other siblings to his maternal grandfather's home. His mother later remarried. He was highly traumatized at age six when his beloved grandfather died of a heart attack. He also viewed the corpse before burial, which added to his trauma.

Growing up, he was aware of his homosexual attractions. In 1961, he joined the British Army after leaving school, and enlisted in the Army Catering Corps. He became a cook, which gave him the chance to learn skills that would later serve him in his killing spree. Eleven years later, he was discharged upon his request. A month later, in December 1972, he joined the Metropolitan Police. There he discovered his fascination with autopsied bodies at the morgue. He resigned after eight months. In November of 1975, he moved into a flat at 195 Melrose Avenue in Cricklewood, London, with roommate David Gallichan, who moved out two years later.

His first murder was on December 30, 1978. He met a young man in a pub and invited him home. To prevent the man from leaving in the morning, he used a tie to strangle him, and then drowned him in a bucket of water. He washed the corpse, put it in his bed, and unsuccessfully attempted to have sex with it. He spent the night sleeping next to his victim. He then hid the body for seven months under his floorboards before burning the remains in the back garden.

On December 3, 1979, he met Canadian tourist Kenneth Ockendon in a pub. After a day of sightseeing and drinking, Nilsen took back Ockendon to his flat, where he strangled him with an electrical cable. Again, he cleaned the corpse, engaged in sex, and spent the night next to it. Then he hid the body under the floorboards, but would constantly remove it to have conversations with, as if Ockendon were still alive.

On May 13, 1980, he met his third victim. Martyn Duffey was a homeless sixteen-year-old that Nilson invited to spend the night. As before, he strangled and drowned his victim, brought him to bed, and masturbated over him. He kept him in a wardrobe for two weeks, and then put him under the floorboards with his previous victim.

The string of victims was growing. In August 1980, Nilsen strangled twenty-seven-year-old Billy Sutherland, a male prostitute. After Sutherland, Nilsen killed eight unidentified victims and stored them under his floorboards. On September 18, 1981, Nilsen killed Malcom Barlow (age twenty-four), an orphan with learning difficulties, by strangling him. He was beginning to run out of hiding places at this point. To get rid of the flies from the decomposing bodies in the flat, he had to spray it twice a day. Nislen convinced his neighbours that the smell was from structural problems. To get rid of the bodies, he began dismembering them, boiling the skulls to remove the flesh, placing the organs in plastic disposable bags, and burning the remains in the back garden, adding an old car tire to the bonfire to disguise the smell.

On October 5, 1981, Nilsen moved to a top-floor flat at 23 Cranley Gardens, in North London. In March of 1982, he murdered John Howlett, and then dismembered the body and flushed the pieces down the toilet. In September 1982, he murdered Archibald Graham Allan (age twenty-seven). His body was left in the bathtub for three days before Nilsen dismembered and disposed of it. On January 26, 1983, he killed his last victim, twenty-year-old Steven Sinclair.

In early February 1983, one of Nilsen's neighbours called a drain specialist. Rotting human remains were discovered blocking the drains and the police were called. Nilsen tried to cover his tracks by removing the remains, but a suspicious tenant spotted him. On February 9, 1983, a detective came to question Nilsen, who calmly confessed and gave details of the murders. He was tried on October 24, 1983, and convicted of six murders and two attempted murders (some men were lucky to escape). He was sentenced to life imprisonment on November 4, 1983.

CHAPTER 31: DENNIS RADER

aka the BTK Killer

'The code word for me will be...Bind them, torture them, kill them, B.T.K." Dennis Rader, the BTK Killer, used these words to end the letter that he had sent to the police in his first attempt of communication.

Dennis Lynn Rader was born on March 9, 1945, and grew up in Wichita. He developed unnatural urges when he was young, and began strangling cats and dogs. In the late 1960s, he joined the Air Force for four years. In 1971, he married Paula Dietz, and later had a son and a daughter with her. For some time, he worked at a firm that installed burglar alarms, which would later help him enter houses undetected. He graduated with a degree in Administration of Justice after six years at night school. Around 1989, he became a city compliance officer.

Dennis Rader planned his attacks very carefully. They were so perfectly planned that he was able to commit the killings in broad daylight. On January 15, 1974, the murders commenced. Prepared, he broke into the Otero family residence. After severing the phone lines, Rader threatened the family with a gun.

Then, he tied up the wrists and ankles of the parents, thirty-eight-year-old Joseph Otero and thirty-three-year-old Julie Otero, and strangled them. The son, nine-year-old Joseph Junior, was taken to the bedroom where he was also tied up and covered in a hood until he suffocated while Dennis watched. The daughter, eleven-year-old Josephine, was taken to the basement and hanged from a pipe. Dennis Rader didn't sexually assault his victims, but when the daughter was dead, he masturbated. Afterwards, he cleaned up any evidence and stole the father's watch as a memento. Charlie, the eldest child, came home from school in the afternoon to find his entire family murdered.

Four months later, Rader, wearing a ski mask, waited for brother and sister, Kevin and Kathryn Bright, to return home. He also threatened them with a gun, claiming that he was a fugitive in need of food and money. He tied them both up in separate rooms. Kevin was shot twice in the head, but somehow survived. Twenty-one-year-old Kathryn struggled, but Rader strangled her and then stabbed her eleven times in the stomach, and left her to bleed out for five hours. That was when he wrote his first letter to the police to claim responsibility for the murders.

On March 17, 1977, he followed a little boy home. He entered the home of twenty-four-year-old Shirley Vian and threatened her with a gun. He told her that he just wanted to tie her up for him to be sexually satisfied. She complied, and confined her three children in the bathroom. He tied her wrists and ankles, and instead of raping her as she expected, he strangled her while her children watched. He wanted to kill the children as well, but the telephone rang and he left in a hurry.

His next victim was Nancy Fox (age twenty-five) whom he killed on December 8, 1977. He handcuffed her, laid her facedown on bed, and strangled her with a nylon stocking. Then, he masturbated. Before leaving, he took her driving license. Later, he called the police to inform them of this murder. He then stopped killing for a number of years.

On April 27, 1985, after careful planning, he strangled his neighbour Marine Hedge (age fifty-three) with pantyhose. Then, he photographed her in sexually explicit poses and dumped the body on a dirt road. On September 16, 1986, he killed Vicki Wegerle (age twenty-eight) after persuading her to let him into her house. she struggled, but he succeeded in tying her up with leather shoelaces. He strangled her with one of her stockings, then rearranged her clothes, and photographed her. In 1991, his known last victim, Dolores "Dee" Davis (age sixty-three), was killed in her home when Rader choked her to death.

The BTK killer continued to send letters to the police about the killings. In 2003, a local lawyer announced that he was writing a biography of the killer. Rader sent a computer disk to the police, and after forensic examination, his church and name were revealed. On February 25, 2005, after thirty-one years of mystery, Rader was arrested. After thorough questioning, he confessed. On June 27, 2005, he was convicted and sentenced to life imprisonment without parole for 175 years.

CHAPTER 32: DONALD HARVEY

It seemed weird, but Donald Harvey was almost always nearby when one of the patients died, thus earning him the nickname the "Angel of Death." This dedicated medical employee would work wherever he was needed and even took night shifts. For years, no one knew that under that angelical face hid a murderer.

Donald Harvey was born in Ohio on April 15, 1952. After his birth, he relocated with his parents to Booneville, Kentucky. Later interviews with his parents and school principal indicated that Harvey had a happy, peaceful childhood. Without much effort, he achieved decent grades. In 1968, he dropped out of high school and got a job in a famous local factory in Ohio. Around 1970, he was laid off. After a few days, his mother called urging him to get back to Kentucky to see his dying grandfather at the Marymount Hospital, so he decided to come back. He spent so much time at the hospital that the nuns working there grew to like him. He was soon offered the job of an orderly there, and he accepted. He changed bedpans, inserted catheters, and passed out medications.

A few months after beginning work at the Marymount Hospital, Harvey found his first victim and committed the first crime of his life. He walked into a patient's private room to check his health condition. The patient had rubbed feces all over his face, which enraged Harvey. He smothered the patient to death and was able to take a shower before reporting the death. No one suspected a thing. Three weeks later, he killed another patient by disconnecting the oxygen supply at the bedside of an elderly woman. That murder also went undetected, so he became more confident about his killings. He killed more than a dozen people within the same year, using several different methods. He used plastic bags, morphine, or other drugs.

His most brutal murder took place when a patient had hit him over the head with a bedpan, thinking he was an intruder. Harvey straightened out a coat hanger and shoved it into the patient's catheter, puncturing his stomach. As a result, the man died days later from an infection.

On March 31, 1971, he was detained for suspicion of burglary. During interrogations, he drunkenly babbled to the policemen about his murders, but there was no evidence so he was only charged for stealing and had to pay a small fine after pleading guilty. He joined the U.S. Air Force, but was discharged in March of 1972. He became depressed, and committed himself into a medical centre several times. He was released in October of 1972, and got another job in a hospital but controlled his urge to kill. During September 1975, he came back to Ohio and got a position in the Cincinnati V.A. Medical Hospital. He worked night shifts as a housekeeping aide, an autopsy assistant, a cardiac-catheterization technician, and a nursing assistant. For ten years, he killed at least fifteen patients using various methods. He would suffocate them with a plastic bag or wet towel, put rat poison or arsenic or cyanide in their food, or inject cyanide into the intravenous tubes or the patients' buttocks. He kept detailed journals about his crimes, while looking at the medical records to help him hide his crimes. He accumulated thirty pounds of cyanide in his house and he would bring portions of it to work to kill patients.

In the 1980s, he moved in with boyfriend Carl Hoeweler and started poisoning him because he feared Carl was cheating on him. Harvey also poisoned his neighbour with hepatitis serums, but she survived. Another neighbour wasn't as lucky when she was poisoned by arsenic and died in the same week. Harvey also poisoned Hoeweler's parents, killing his father and making his mother ill. When Carl left him, he attempted to get his revenge by poisoning him a final time, but fortunately, the victim survived. In another job at Cincinnati's Drake Memorial Hospital in 1986, Harvey killed twenty-three patients in thirteen months.

In April 1987, authorities became suspicious of Harvey after the death of John Powell, a comatose patient starting to recover. Further investigation led them to the "Angel of Death," Donald Harvey. Police obtained a warrant to search his apartment, where they found loads of evidence against him. He was arrested and he confessed to the murders. The following year, he was sentenced to life in prison without parole before the year 2047.

CHAPTER 33: DONALD HENRY GASKINS

One of the most brutal and prolific serial killers in the last century was Donald Henry Gaskins. Killing when rejected, when hurt, or just for fun, Donald Gaskins had a large number of victims, and the total body count is still unknown today.

Born in South Carolina on March 13, 1933, Donald Henry "Pee Wee" Gaskins, Jr. had a difficult childhood. His mother lived with different men who abused him. When she got married, his stepfather also beat him up and abused him. Due to his small size for his age, he had the nickname "Pee Wee." He wouldn't learn or even hear his real given name spoken until it was read in his first court appearance.

During his school years, Gaskins frequently fought with his classmates and was punished by his teachers. At age eleven, he quit school and began working at a garage with two other boys, Danny and Marsh, and they would become known as "The Trouble Trio." They began burglarizing and raping other boys. Once they were caught gang raping Marsh's sister by Marsh's parents, so the parents broke up the group after beating them up until they bled. Now Donald was alone in his life of crime. When he was thirteen, he was caught stealing by a woman, so he hit her with an axe. She survived and he was sent to reform school for punishment. There, he was constantly abused and raped, and to survive he had to offer sex for protection. When he was eighteen, married and with a child, a teenage girl accused him of insurance fraud, so he hit her with a hammer. He was later sentenced to six years in prison for attempted murder, and his wife divorced him.

He committed his first murder in prison at the age of twenty. He slashed an inmate's throat to show he was not an easy target. He escaped prison but was arrested again. In 1963, he was sentenced to five years and then paroled after raping a twelve-year-old girl. This was when his killing spree began.

Gaskins divided his killings into two types: "weekend recreation" and "serious murders." In the first type, he would kill randomly. For example, once a female hitchhiker laughed at his sex offer, so he beat her till she was unconscious, then raped her, sodomized her, mutilated her, and then drowned her in a swamp. Along the coast, he killed again and again. He would keep his victims alive for as long as possible so he could torture them. He mutilated his victims, stabbed, and suffocated them. There were times when he would eat some of their flesh in front of them, and force them to have bites too.

The second type of killings, what Gaskins referred to as "serious murders," were when he would kill people he knew. In November 1970, he tried to sexually assault his niece, Janice Kirby (age fifteen), and her friend. Then, he beat them to death. He would also kill people who owed him money or had insulted him. These murders were executions and not fun torture. Another victim was an old friend of his, twenty-two-year-old Doreen Dempsey, who was pregnant and a mother of a two-year-old girl. She asked Gaskin for a lift, he accepted and asked for sex in exchange. She accepted, but when he asked the same of her daughter, she refused. So he raped and killed her, and did the same to her daughter.

He later also became a killer for hire. He was hired many times to kill, but required help with the burying of the victims, which would later lead to his arrest.

One of his criminal colleagues, who once helped in burying the victims, claimed that he saw Donald murder two men. After the disappearance of Kim Ghelkins (age thirteen), the evidence led the police to Gaskins. During questioning, he confessed to his murders. On December 4, 1975, Gaskins took police to some land he owned where he had buried some of his victims. On May 24, 1976, he was found guilty of the murders and was sentenced to death. While in prison, he was hired to kill fellow inmate Rudolph Tyner for revenge, which he succeeded in doing. In an attempt to avoid the electric chair, he slit his wrists on the day of execution. However, he survived and was executed on September 6, 1991.

CHAPTER 34: DR. JACK KEVORKIAN

aka Dr. Death

Doctors are known for making patients feel better, for helping them get through illnesses and diseases, and sometimes even for prolonging their lives. In early 1990s, a doctor emerged who would help patients to get better by ending their lives. Dr. Death claimed that he provided merciful death.

Born Murad Kevorkian on May 26, 1928, he was later known as Jack Kevorkian. His parents were Armenian refugees who barely escaped the Armenian massacres after World War I. He was the middle child and had two sisters. Although they weren't rich, his parents worked hard to provide for the family. However, they were strict religious parents, and the children were forced to attend church. Growing up, Jack had many questions. He debated the idea of God's existence, wondering if there really was a God, then why he would allow the slaughter of his entire extended family. By age twelve, he still couldn't find the answers and he stopped to go to church.

At school, the three children demonstrated high

academic intelligence, especially Jack. As a young boy, he loved to read, draw, paint, and play the piano; he excelled in everything. He also had a critical mind, and would often fall into debates with his teachers. Being this much academically advanced made it hard for him to make friends. During his spare time, he only focused on his studies. At the age of seventeen, he graduated with honours from Pontiac High School.

He wanted to become a civil engineer, but soon began focusing on botany and biology. In 1952, he graduated in medicine at the University of Michigan, and then specialized in pathology. When the Korean War started, he served fifteen months as an Army medical officer in Korea, and finished his service in Colorado. In his years as a resident, he became fascinated by death. He would take pictures of terminally ill patients to help determine the exact moment of death. He presented a paper to the American Association for the Advancement of Science with the idea of experimenting on criminals on death row, but was denied, and ejected from the University of Michigan Medical Center. It was at that time that earned the nickname "Dr. Death" by his peers.

He continued his internship at Pontiac General Hospital. He had an idea to make blood transfusions from a dead corpse to a living human as a way to help if there was a deficiency in the blood bank. This idea resulted in him being considered an outsider, and later Kevorkian was infected with Hepatitis C. In 1986, he heard that doctors in the Netherlands were assisting in the death of people by lethal injection. He then created a suicide machine he called the "Thanatron" to help the terminally ill with suicide. The machine consisted of three bottles: first a saline solution, followed by a pain-killer, and finally a fatal dose of the poison potassium chloride.

His first death was Janet Adkins (age forty-five). She asked for his help to end her life using the "Thana-tron" after she learned that she had Alzheimer's disease. He was charged with murder after her death, but the charge was dismissed because Michigan's laws at that time were not clear on euthanasia. From then on, he continued his assisted suicide activities, while simultaneously fighting the legal aspect. By the time a law was enacted, making the act of helping someone commit suicide illegal, and Jack was arrested, he had helped more than 130 patients to their death.

Nothing would stop Jack from continuing his helpings, so in 1998 he gave CBS's *60 Minutes* program a tape of him assisting a patient with Lou Gehrig's disease to end his life. Following the broadcast footage, the prosecutors charged him with second-degree murder. On March 26, 1999, he was found guilty and was sentenced to twenty-five years in prison with the possibility of parole. On June 1, 2007, he was released on good behaviour. He began giving lectures about assisted suicide. On June 3, 2011, when Jack was eighty-three years old, he died in Michigan at Beaumont Hospital, two weeks after his hospitalization because of heart and kidney problems.

CHAPTER 35:
ED GEIN

In the late 1950s, in a farm in Plainfield, Wisconsin, police found human remains used as decorations. It seemed as if the owner had been, for years, exhuming bodies from the graveyard and collecting trophies. In addition to the exhumed corpses, the bodies of two local murdered women were also found.

Edward Theodore Gein was born in La Crosse, Wisconsin, on August 27, 1906. He had a brother, Henry, who was older than he by seven years. His father was an alcoholic, and his mother a domineering religious Lutheran. Ed's mother told her children that every woman, other than her, was a prostitute and the instrument of evil; drinking was dangerous too. She never thought much of her boys, telling them that would account for nothing. Edward was shy and not very social, especially since his mother punished him every time he tried to make friends.

On April 1, 1940, his father died of heart failure caused by alcoholism. On May 16, 1944, Ed and his brother were burning away marsh vegetation on the property when the fire raged out of control. The local fire-extinguishing department came to help them. Henry went missing during the chaos, and after extensive searching, he was found dead. The cause of his death appeared to be suffocation and heart failure, although there was a bruise on Henry's head. The truth about what really happened was never determined. After Henry's death, Ed's mother suffered a stroke that left her paralyzed. Ed cared for her, but her health was constantly declining and she died on December 29, 1945. Ed was devastated by his mother's death; it was like he went crazy afterwards and became obsessed with everything related to death.

Ed later befriended a gravedigger, Gus, whom he persuaded to help him dig up bodies from the graveyard. Ed removed strips of skin, genitalia, whole breasts, and even entire bodies and took the parts home as trophies. Then he began searching for freshly buried corpses of older women who resembled his mother, exhumed their bodies, and took the skin. He created morbid trophies, like a human skull he used as a soup bowl; shirts, lampshades, and chair coverings made of human skin; a curtain pull with a woman's lips sewed into it; a belt studded with female nipples; nine women's faces that he hung on the wall... However, in 1954, his partner Gus was put in a home, no longer assisting him with the exhumations, so he had to create his own dead bodies.

His first murder was committed on December 8, 1954. Mary Hogan was the owner of the local tavern. Ed was a customer there. She disappeared under mysterious circumstances. Ed wasn't suspected although he jokingly said that she stayed overnight with him but no one believed him.

On November 16, 1957, Bernice Worden, who was the owner of a hardware store, also disappeared.

Her son informed the investigators that Ed was a customer that evening and had promised to return a gallon of antifreeze in the morning. It was discovered that a receipt for the antifreeze was the last receipt written by the victim before her disappearance. Investigators obtained a warrant to search Ed's farm, and were horrified by what they found. In addition to the human trophies collected over the years, investigators also found Bernice's decapitated and naked body hung upturned by ropes at her wrists. She was killed with a .22 caliber pistol and mutilated postmortem.

Ed Gein was arrested and taken to Wautoma County jail. At first, he denied everything, but he eventually he confessed to all his crimes: the exhumations and the murders of both Hogan and Worden.

During the interrogation, the Sheriff beat up Ed, which ultimately made his confession inadmissible. Ed was evaluated by psychiatrists and was declared unfit for the trial, so he was committed to the Central State Hospital in Waupun, Wisconsin. In November 1968, he was declared mentally competent for trial for the murder of Bernice Worden. He was found not guilty by reason of insanity and sent back to Central State hospital in Waupun.

CHAPTER 36:
EDMUND KEMPER

aka The Co-ed Killer

"I just wondered how it would feel to shoot Grandma." That's what a fifteen-year-old boy with a troubled childhood said after murdering both of his grandparents. They weren't his only killings.

Edmund Emil "Big Ed" Kemper III was born on December 18, 1948, in Burbank, California. When he was only nine years old, his parents got divorced and his father left. He was left with his two sisters and his mother, an alcoholic, who constantly belittled him, telling him that no woman would ever love him. His mother often verbally abused him. She sometimes locked him in the basement out of fear that he would rape his younger sister. Edmund grew up hating himself, resenting men because of his father, and hating women because of his mother. As a game, he pretended that he was being executed in a gas chamber. He began decapitating his sister's dolls at home, and then moved on to bury his cat alive when he was only ten. When the cat died, he dug it up, decapitated it, and displayed it on a spike as his trophy. When he was thirteen, he sliced another cat open with a machete, showering in the cat's blood. Edmund often fantasized about killing the people in his town and then having sex with their dead bodies. He grew up to be a large man with a high IQ.

When he was fifteen, he was sent to live with his grandparents on a ranch in California. During his first summer there, on August 27, 1964, he killed his grandmother and stabbed her many times. When Edmund's grandfather got home, he shot him too. He then called his mother and the police to come arrest him. He was sent to the State Hospital after being diagnosed with paranoid schizophrenia. There, he listened to serial rapists recount their crime stories, and he enjoyed it. Five years later, he was paroled and then released to his mother's care.

Edmund's killing spree took place between May 1972 and February 1973. On May 7, 1972, he picked up two eighteen-year-old students, Anita Luchessa and Mary Ann Pesce. He took them to an isolated area where he smothered and stabbed Pesce and also stabbed Luchessa. He then took them to his apartment, decapitated them, had oral sex with the heads, and then dumped the body parts. On September 14, 1972, he picked up fifteen-year-old Aiko Koo on her way to the dance class. He strangled her and then had sex with her dead body on the side of the road. On January 7, 1973, he picked up nineteen-year-old Cindy Schall. In a secluded wooded area, he shot her with a .22 caliber gun, brought her to his mother's home, dismembered her, buried her head in the backyard, and then got rid of the rest of the parts. On February 5 of the same year, he kidnapped Rosalind Thorpe (age twenty-four) and Alice Liu (age twenty-three). He then shot them with the same .22 caliber gun and sexually abused their bodies. The next day he dismembered them, and dumped the remains in Eden Canyon, where they were found a week later. All these murders happened after an argument between Edmund and his mother.

On April 20, 1973, he beat his own mother to death with a claw hammer in her room. Then he decapitated her and used her severed head for oral sex and then as a dartboard. He cut out her vocal cords and put them in the garbage disposal, which ejected the tissues back up into the sink. Later that night, he invited his mother's best friend over for dinner. He then strangled fifty-nine-year-old Sally Hallett to death and violated her body before leaving the crime scene.

Edmund fled and made it to Colorado. He realized that the last crime would be linked to him, so he decided to confess. He called the police and confessed to the eight murders. At first, they didn't believe him, but he was ultimately arrested. He pleaded not guilty by reason of insanity, but was ultimately determined to be legally sane. He was convicted for the murders and sentenced to life imprisonment. He was sent to California Medical Facility, where he remains to this day.

CHAPTER 37: FERNANDO HERNANDEZ LEYVA

"I killed them because I had to, I don't know how to do anything else." This was the reason that Fernando Hernandez gave for killing over 100 people. This merciless serial killer murdered for pleasure only, and nothing else.

Fernando Hernandez Leyva was born in Cuernavaca, Morelos, Mexico in 1964. Little is known about his childhood and the life that he led. It was not yet known what exactly made him commit all these killings. Over a period of thirteen years, he was arrested twice. In both instances, he escaped. First in 1982, he was arrested in Cuernavaca on robbery charges and he escaped by tunneling through a wall. In 1986, he was arrested the second time on suspicion of murder and robbery and he escaped again. On March 24, 1999, he was arrested for a third time. This time he didn't try to escape; instead, he tried to commit suicide on April 10,

1999. However, due to his weight (300 pounds; around 130 kg), the rope he was using to hang himself broke and he fell. He suffered from minor injuries in his neck.

No one was able to believe when the Mexican police announced that they had arrested a man wanted in four states, and responsible for the death of dozens of persons and six kidnappings. As the investigation continued, the number of victims grew significantly until it reached about 137 murders. His victims were selected randomly. At first, he confessed to the murders. He later retracted his confession, saying that he had only kidnapped a journalist (Carlos Cabello Wallace in September 1996) and killed a police officer. He claimed that the police had beat him and threatened to rape his wife and take his children if he didn't confess. The authorities never publically commented to dispute Leyva's claims.

Fernando Hernandez Leyva was evaluated by psychiatrists, and was found to be a psychopath who committed murders for his own satisfaction. Dozens of police cars protected him from the angry crowd as he was transferred to a state prison. The police presence was heavy, prohibiting him from trying to escape as he had done twice before.

Leyva was tried and sentenced to life imprisonment, since there is no death penalty in Mexico. Currently, he is serving his sentence in the prison of La Palma, under strict supervision.

CHAPTER 38: FRED WEST

Fred was a son, a brother, a husband, a father, a rapist, and a murderer.

Frederick Walter Stephen West was born on September 29, 1941 to a poor family. He was the second oldest of six children. Fred claimed that his father had been sexually intimate with his sister, and he had taught him bestiality. It has been suspected but never confirmed that his mother had sexually abused him starting at age twelve. He left school when he was fifteen. At the age of seventeen, he got into an accident that left him with a fractured skull, a broken arm, and broken leg, which became shorter than the other. He was in a coma for seven days and underwent an operation to place a metallic plate in his head.

After his accident, it was reported that he had sudden episodes of rage and anger. Two years later, he hit his head again, which resulted in him being unconscious for a whole day. When he was nineteen, he was arrested while molesting a thirteen-year-old girl. He was convicted for the crime, but was able to escape imprisonment. His family disowned him and sent him to live with his aunt.

In September 1962, Fred resumed his relationship with his ex-girlfriend Catherine Rena Costello when she was working as a prostitute and already pregnant. Two months later, they got married. On February 22, 1963, Charmaine Carol was born. Another daughter, Anne Marie, was born in July of 1964. On November 4, 1965, while working as an ice cream van driver, Fred hit and killed a four-year-old boy. The family was forced to move to Gloucestershire along with Isa McNeill, the nanny caring for the children, and Anne McFall, Catherine's friend. In 1966, Catherine and Isa left and moved to Scotland escaping Fred's "weird" sexual demands, but Anne stayed, along with the two children. Later, Fred and Anne began a relationship.

In August 1967, Anne, who was eight months pregnant, disappeared. Her remains wouldn't be found until June of 1994.

On November 29, 1968, Fred met Rosemary Letts. A year later, on her sixteenth birthday, they moved into a two-story house together. On October 17, 1970, Rosemary gave birth to their daughter, Heather Ann. Shortly after, Fred was arrested for theft, and was imprisoned until June 24, 1971. Just before Fred was released, Rosemary killed Charmaine. Two months after Fred's release, Catherine came back for her daughters, and the couple killed her too. On January 29, 1972, Fred and Rosemary got married, and on June 1, they had their second daughter, Mae. Fred then encouraged his wife to become a prostitute, and she would later have seven children—three of mixed race and one who may have been fathered by Rosemary's own father. The couple raped and tortured many young women, one of them Caroline Roberts on December

6, 1972, and even their own daughters, such as Fred's eight-year-old daughter, Anne Marie.

Fred's victims were mostly females. He killed women related to him, women he knew, women he hired as nannies, or women he had lured into to the house somehow. Fred and Rosemary would subdue them, rape and torture them, then strangle them to death or suffocate them. After the victims were dead, Fred would cut off their fingers and toes, and sometimes their kneecaps before burying them.

Fred started abusing Heather after Anne Marie left the house. Heather then told some friends about what was really going on in the house. Once the couple learned of this, they decided to kill her. In June of 1987, they strangled sixteen-year-old Heather, dismembered her, and buried her in the garden. They would later tell the other children to behave or they would "end up under the patio like Heather."

In May of 1992, Fred recorded himself raping one of his daughters. She told her friends about the incident, and one of her friends told her mother, who went to the police. An investigation into the rapes began, and the couple was eventually charged. However, the case couldn't move forward and the charges were dropped because the witnesses refused to come forward and testify. Investigators persisted and continued to look into Heather's disappearance, issuing a search warrant for the residence. While excavating the garden, human bones were discovered. On February 25, 1994, Fred was arrested and he confessed to his crimes. He was charged with eleven murders, and the murder of Anne McFall was added to his rap sheet on July 3, 1994, after her body was found later. On January 1, 1995, Fred hanged himself in his cell.

CHAPTER 39:
FRIEDRICH FRITZ
HAARMANN

After World War I, Germany experienced some difficult times. Hanover was one of the cities the most affected by famine and deprivation. On May 17, 1924, some children were playing near a river close to Herrenhausen Castle, where they found a human skull. Twelve days later, another skull was found on the riverbank. On June 13, two more skulls washed up. The victims were between the ages of eighteen and twenty, and one boy of twelve years old. It became apparent to the authorities that a killer had emerged.

Friedrich Heinrich Karl "Fritz" Haarmann was born October 25, 1879, in Hanover. His was family was poor, and he had five other siblings. Even as a young boy, he always preferred to use his sisters' toys instead of engaging in boys' activities. He didn't perform well in school, so at the age of sixteen, he enrolled in a military academy in Neu Breisach. He did well, but a year later was discharged after suffering from seizures. He returned to his town and started working in a cigarette factory. In 1898, he was accused of molesting children. After being declared mentally unfit for trial, he was sent to a mental institution. He escaped to Switzerland after two months, and didn't come back until around the year 1900. He again enrolled in the military under a pseudonym, but in October of 1901, was again rusticated due to medical conditions. After a violent fight with his father, he was arrested but discharged. He opened a business of his own but it soon it went bankrupt.

His criminal career began as he became a trivial thief and a con artist, and spent the next decade in and out of prison. He became known to the Hanover police, and later became an informant. After some time, the police considered him to be an ideal source for information, which made it easier for him to redirect them from his activities. The state of the country after World War I made it easier for criminals to operate.

On September 25, 1918, seventeen-year-old Friedel Rothe disappeared. He was last spotted with Fritz. The police were urged to arrest him by the community, and when they raided his apartment, they saw him in bed with another boy, so they charged him for sexual assault. Haarmann received nine months of imprisonment for this crime. After being released, he met Hans Grans who later became his lover, and they moved in together as Fritz continued killing others.

Fritz's victims were young men, usually runaways or male prostitutes. He usually lured them from Hanover's Central Station into his apartment, and killed them by biting their throats. Some of the victims were killed while he sodomized them. He was later dubbed as the Vampire of Hanover. After he murdered his victims, he would dismember them and threw the remains in the River Leine. He stole his victims' possessions and either sold them in the black market or kept them in the home he shared with his lover. There was a rumour that Fritz actually canned his victims' meat and sold it in the black market, but this could never be confirmed. Hans became an accomplice to the murders, and even asked Fritz to kill more.

Aside from Friedel Rothe, in 1923, Fritz killed thirteen men between the ages of thirteen and nineteen, and in 1924, another thirteen men between the ages of ten and twenty years old. As a trusted informant, he wasn't suspected of the murders.

The remains that Fritz had dumped in the river were eventually discovered. Five hundred human bones were discovered, which were believed to belong to twenty-two different victims. Finally, Fritz was considered a suspect, since he had a history of sexually harassing children, and was already linked to the kidnapping of Friedel Rothe, his first victim in 1918. Fritz was put under surveillance, and was seen stalking boys at the Central Station on June 22, 1924. He was immediately arrested for luring a boy into his apartment, which investigators searched thoroughly. Police found bloodstains and possessions of earlier victims as well. He was interrogated, and confessed to raping and killing young males since 1918. He claimed that he had killed between fifty and seventy people, but investigators were only able to link him to twenty-seven murders.

On December 4, 1924, the trial began, and on December 19, he was found guilty of twenty-four murders and sentenced to death. His accomplice, Hans, was sentenced to twelve years. On April 15, 1925, Fritz was beheaded by guillotine.

CHAPTER 40:
GARY RIDGWAY

Sixteen-year-old Gary lured a six-year-old boy into the woods. He stabbed him in the ribs and walked away laughing. He later said, "I always wondered what it would be like to kill someone." The boy survived, but Gary was never arrested for this crime.

Gary Leon Ridgway was born on February 18, 1949, in Utah. He had two brothers. When he was nine, the family moved to Washington. His parents often argued violently and his mother was domineering. Gary, as a boy, was a bed-wetter. Whenever he wet his bed, she would clean him up, and then embarrass him in front of his father and brothers. At an early age, Gary was killing and torturing animals.

At school, Gary performed poorly. He had an IQ of 82. Once, he had to repeat a year twice in high school so he could get a passing grade. He graduated when he was twenty-one, and soon married a high school girlfriend, Claudia Barrows. He enlisted in the Navy and served in Vietnam aboard a supply ship. During this time, he started spending time with prostitutes. His marriage ended one year later when his wife had an affair.

In December 1973, he got married again, to Marcia Winslow, and they had a son two years later. During his second marriage, he became very religious, reading the Bible and urging his wife to follow the teaching of their church's pastor. This marriage also ended due to infidelities. Gary demanded sex frequently, even in public places. He was simultaneously torn between his lusts and his religious beliefs. In 1988, he married a third time, to a woman named Judith Mawson. During their time together, he felt less of an urge to kill. They were still together when he was finally arrested.

Gary's victims were mostly prostitutes and runaways. He would pick them up and drive them to his home or to a secluded area. He would put them at ease when talking affectionately with them, sometimes showing them a picture of his son before having sex with them. When they finished, he strangled the women. At first, he used his bare hands to strangle the women, but when the victims began inflicting suspicious defense wounds on him, he started using ligatures. Once the women were dead, he dumped them someplace where he could later return and re-live the experience, and sometimes have sex with their bodies again. His first victims were dumped in the Green River, thus earning him his nickname the Green River Killer. To divert the police, he threw things belonging to other women at the dumpsites, or even drove the bodies across the state line into Oregon. Most of the murders happened between 1982 and 1983. He killed at least seventy women this way.

When the first bodies were found, Gary was a person of interest, but police couldn't find enough evidence to convict him. He took a polygraph test twice and passed. Even serial killer Ted Bundy, who was on death row at the time in 1984, was helping the police by giving them his opinion about the psychology and motives of the murderer. He suggested when the police found a fresh grave, they should stake it out because he believed the killer would return. DNA samples were taken from Gary in 1987, but wouldn't prove helpful until 2001, when new technology was used to link the murders to him.

On November 30, 2001, Gary Ridgway was arrested. The DNA testing finally linked him to the murders of Opal Mills, Marcia Chapman, Carol Ann Christensen, and Cynthia Hinds. He was found connected to three more victims, Debra Bonner, Debra Estes, and Wendy Coffield, after the spheres of microscopic spray paint on the victims were identified with the same composition and brand of paint that had been used in the Kenworth factory where Gary was working at the exact time frame of these murders.

As a part of his plea bargain and to escape the death penalty, Gary confessed to the murders of seventy-one women, and helped lead the police to where he dumped them. It was suspected that his victim count was actually much higher. He was charged with forty-nine murders, and sentenced to life imprisonment without parole. He is currently serving his sentence at the Washington State Penitentiary in Walla Walla, Washington.

CHAPTER 41: GERALD EUGENE STANO

On Sunday, February 17, 1980, two drunken students stumbled onto what appeared to be the decomposing body of a young lady. Detective Sergeant Paul Crow started the investigation and soon learned the body was that of twenty-year-old Mary Carol Maher. It appeared that she had been stabbed multiple times in the back, chest, and legs, and then the killer had posed her body. Other victims were soon also discovered.

Born on September 12, 1951, Paul Zeininger was neglected as a young infant. His birth mother didn't much care for him, and when he was just six months old, she gave him up for adoption. The country doctors declared him "unadoptable" when they saw he was ingesting his own feces, and described his functioning as at "an animalistic level." Despite all this, Paul was able to find a loving home with Nurse Norma Stano, who renamed him Gerald Eugene Stano. Stano loved Gerald, but they had a problem with discipline. Throughout his school years, he only excelled in music; as for the rest of his courses, he earned Cs and Ds. He was a bed-wetter until the age of ten.

Gerald was also a compulsive liar and a petty thief. Once, he was caught stealing money from his father to pay the members on his track and field team to let him finish first. He mostly hung out alone, and became a target for bullies and a joke for girls. He didn't graduate high school until he was twenty-one, and didn't attend college after. Throughout his adolescent years, his parents kept trying to set him straight without success. He continued to steal from classmates, and later coworkers, and was arrested several times but never convicted.

Gerald claimed that he began killing as soon as he was eighteen years old. His victims were women, and he killed them by stabbing. Wherever he moved, girls went missing in the area of his residence. However, there wasn't any physical evidence to charge him with the murders. He killed most of his victims when he was living in Florida and New Jersey.

On March 25, 1980, a prostitute went to the police station and reported an incident to Detective Jim Gadberry. She explained that a man driving a red Gremlin had picked her up, and when they went to a motel room, he refused to pay her. They argued, and the man sliced open the right side of her thigh with a knife, and fled. She received twenty-seven stitches to close the wound. She said that she could identify the man if she saw him, and was certain that his car would be present at the building of a local apartment. Detective Gadberry drove towards the apartment building and spotted the car parked about a mile away. He ran the license plate, and found that it belonged to twenty-eight-year-old Gerald. He noticed that Gerald had been arrested many times but never convicted. When he showed his picture to the prostitute, she identified him as the person who assaulted her. Gerald was arrested, and after thorough questioning, he admitted to the assault.

In the meantime, Detective Sergeant Crow noticed that Gerald fit the profile of the man who committed the murders. He asked for a chance to interrogate him. After studying his reactions and knowing when Gerald would be lying, Crow was able to question him successfully. Gerald finally confessed to the murder of Mary Carol Maher. However, there was a question lingering: had Gerald committed other crimes? Crow went through the missing persons cases, and started the interrogation again.

Gerald knew that in order to escape the death penalty, he would have to arrange a plea bargain. To avoid a long court battle, the prosecutors accepted a guilty plea for the murders of Toni Van Haddocks, Nancy Heard, and Mary Carol Maher in exchange for life sentences. Always one to enjoy the limelight, Gerald eventually confessed to the murders of forty-one women. He pleaded guilty again, and was sentenced to death by electric chair. After stalling the execution with appeals, and one delay due to a malfunctioning with the electric chair, Gerald was finally executed on March 23, 1998.

However, there are some who believe that Gerald didn't really commit all forty-one murders, but instead was fed the details for the confessions by Detective Crow.

CHAPTER 42: GERARD SCHAEFER

In November 1972, seventeen-year-old Susan Place and sixteen-year-old Georgia Jessup disappeared while hitchhiking. Six months later, in April of the following year, their bodies were found. Curiously, the manner in which they were found, tied to a tree, resembled an attempted murder that had occurred in July 1972.

Gerard John Schaefer, Jr. was born on March 25, 1946. He was the eldest of three children born to Gerard and Doris Schaefer. He believed that his parents favoured his sister, and did not get along with them. In 1960, he moved with his family to Florida. During his teen years, Gerard became obsessed with woman's panties and had a tendency for stealing them. He also became a peeping Tom, often spying on his neighbours. In addition, he killed animals for fun, and cross-dressed. He graduated high school in 1964, and went on to earn an associate degree in business administration. In 1968, he became a teacher but was fired a few weeks later for "totally inappropriate behaviour," in the principal's words. He got married that year, but divorced two years later. After getting fired, he tried to become a priest, but was rejected. In 1971, he got married again. Later, he acquired a law enforcement job, and then became a Deputy Sheriff.

On July 21, 1972, Gerard was on patrol. He picked up two hitchhiking girls, eighteen-year-old Pamela Wells and seventeen-year-old Nancy Trotter. He took them to the woods, and tied them to a tree and threatened to kill them. Luckily for the girls, Gerard got a call on his police radio and had to go, but promised to return. During his time gone, the girls were able to escape and get to the nearest police station, which, ironically, was Gerard's station, and report him. When he returned to the woods, he found that they were gone, so he called his boss saying that he had done a foolish thing and he would be mad at him if he saw it. He explained that his attempt was to scare the girls into avoiding such irresponsible way of travelling, but the Sheriff didn't believe him, and he was stripped of his badge, arrested, and charged with assault and unlawful imprisonment. He was released on bail, and in October 1973 was sentenced to one year in prison with the possibility of being released in six months.

Two months later, and before his sentence for assault, he murdered Susan Place and Georgia Jessup. Their bodies weren't found until April 1973, decomposing and butchered. The way in which they were murdered was similar to the way Gerard had attempted to murder Wells and Trotter. Because of this, the police obtained a search warrant of Gerard's home. There, they found stories that Gerard had written describing the torture, rape, and murder of women. Moreover, they found personal possessions linked to at least eight missing victims, including Leigh Hainline, Gerard's neighbour whom he used to peep on when he was a teenager.

Gerard was charged with the murders of Susan Place and Georgia Jessup. He was tried, and in October 1973, he was found guilty of the murders and sentenced to two counts of life imprisonment. He was linked to thirty cases of missing women and girls. Among his other victims were Mary Briscolina and Elsie Farmer (both aged fourteen), who vanished hitchhiking a few weeks after the murder of Place and Jessup. The two girls were raped, killed, and hung from the "Devil's Tree" in Port Saint Lucie. He often bragged about his killings, but threatened to sue anyone who called him a serial killer.

Gerard tried to appeal his sentence many times, but never succeeded. On December 3, 1995, he was found dead in his own cell at the hands of fellow inmate, Vincent Rivera. He was found guilty for Gerard's murder and received an additional fifty-three years on top of his sentence. During his time in prison, Gerard wrote many short murder stories; some described murders he may have committed, and some were fiction. His writings became popular among the crime story enthusiasts, but these writings could give potential criminals ideas on how to commit their own crimes. So, in my opinion, they must be banned.

CHAPTER 43: GILBERT PAUL JORDAN

On February 3, 2005, the Saanich Police Department (in Vancouver, British Colombia, on the West Coast of Canada) issued an alert to warn the public about a recently released convict, Gilbert Jordan, who was known as the "Boozing Barber." The reason behind this alert dated back to Jordan's history of manslaughter and assault.

Gilbert Paul Jordan was born in Vancouver on December 12, 1931. He dropped out of high school at the age of sixteen. Before he hit twenty years old, his criminal record already included assault, rape, theft, car theft, drunk driving, hit and run, and even heroin possession. He was a heavy drinker, and soon he was drinking fifty ounces of vodka every day. Surely, he would always be in the company of other alcoholics. He used to spend time with prostitutes, too. In 1961, he abducted a five-year-old girl. He was charged with kidnapping but never convicted. In December of 1961, while drunk, he stopped traffic by threatening to jump off the Lion's Gate Bridge, but later gave himself up. He saluted the judge Nazi-style, and was found guilty of contempt of the court. Almost two years later, he invited two women into his car for a drink, which led to him being charged with rape and theft, but he was only convicted of theft.

In 1965, Ivy Rose was found naked and dead in a hotel in Vancouver. After testing, the alcohol level in her blood was found to be 0.51; however, no charges were made and her death was declared accidental. Gilbert was charged several times for sexual assault but he wasn't convicted until 1974, and even then, he only served two years in prison. Not long after his release, he was charged again for kidnapping a mentally impaired woman and raping her. He was only sentenced to two years and two months. During his incarceration, he learned a profession, and opened a barbershop upon his release. His shop was close to Hastings Street, near many bars in which Gilbert prowled to stalk and lure his victims.

Apart from Ivy Rose, Gilbert was linked to the death of six other Aboriginal women. Most of them were alcoholics, so he would lure them by offering them a drink. He would make them drink until they pass out, and then keep pouring vodka down their throats until they died from alcohol poisoning. His victims included Mary Johnson, who was killed on November 30, 1980 at the Aylmer Hotel—she was found with a blood alcohol level of .34, and Barbara Paul, killed on September 11, 1981, at the Glenaird Hotel with a blood alcohol level of .41. The following three victims were all found in Gilbert's barbershop: Mary Johns, who was killed on July 30, 1982, found with a blood alcohol level of .76; Patricia Thomas, killed on

December 15, 1984, found with a blood alcohol level of .51; Patricia Andrew, who was killed on June 28, 1985, found with a blood alcohol level of .79; and Vera Harry, killed on November 19, 1986, at the Clifton Hotel, found with a blood alcohol level of .04.

Another victim was Vanessa Lee Buckner. She was found naked in the Niagara hotel on October 12, 1987. It is not really known if she was an alcoholic or not. However, police are certain that Gilbert Jordan was with her the night she died. His fingerprints were found, linking him to her death. A month later, at another hotel, Edna Shade was also found. Between October 12 and November 26, 1987, the police put Gilbert under surveillance. They watched him trying to lure Aboriginal women, and saved four women from becoming his victims.

In 1988, he was tried and found guilty of manslaughter in the death of Vanessa Lee Buckner. He was sentenced to fifteen years, but upon appeal, the sentence was reduced to nine years. He only served six years and then was released and placed on probation. In 2002, he was arrested again for breach of probation, and again on August 11, 2004. After his release, the police issued a public warning cautioning people to be careful around him. In 2006, Gilbert Jordan died.

CHAPTER 44: GILLES DE RAIS

Gilles de Rais was born in the year 1405 at Champtoce-sur-Loire, in a family castle. His parents were Guy II and Marie de Craon de Montmorency-Laval. As a child, he was very intelligent, able to speak Latin fluently. He studied both military discipline and moral development. After the death of his parents in 1415, he and his brother were given to their motherly grandfather. On November 30, 1420, his grandfather arranged for him to get married to Brittany's Catherine de Thouars, who was the heiress of Poitou and La Vendee.

This increased his fortune. The couple had only one child, Marie, who was born in the year 1429. Rais was able to save Duke John VI, who had been taken as a prisoner. To this act, he was rewarded generously with land grants converted later to monetary rewards. In 1425, he learned courtly manners after being brought in to the Charles VII's court. In the battle of Chateau of Lude, he killed Blackburn, the English captain. From the year 1427 to 1435, he was serving as the commander of the Royal army. He displayed acts of reckless bravery. In 1429, Rais fought with Joan of Arc against the English. In the admiration of carrying the Holy Ampulla to Notre-Dame de Reims, he was chosen as a lord (only four were chosen) on July 17, 1429. He was also officially appointed as the Marshal of France. He wasn't present at the burning of Joan of Arc at the stake. Gilles was spending the fortune recklessly, and when his grandfather passed away, he left his sword to Gilles's younger brother.

From the year 1434 to 1435, he withdrew from his military career to pursue the building of a Chapel for the Holy Innocents, and the production of a play. Gilles almost went bankrupt, and began selling his properties. On July 2, 1435, a royal decree was issued to stop him from selling more properties, under the pressure of his family. When he left Orleans, he was required to leave his possessions behind to his creditors.

His assault on children happened between spring 1432 and spring 1433. There are no accounts of his early murders. His first registered case of kidnapping and murdering was that of a twelve-year-old boy named Jeudon, when Gilles moved to Machecoul. There, he sodomized and murdered an uncertain number of children. In 1437, forty bodies were found.

Gilles took the children and hung them with a rope from a hook so they wouldn't cry. Then, he would masturbate on their thighs or belly. Later, he would comfort them, then either kill them himself or order his cousin Gilles de Sille, or a body servant, to kill them. They would be decapitated, have their throats cut, dismembered, and have their necks broken. Gilles de Rais abused his victims before and sometimes after they were dead.

After the children were dead, he kissed them, and admired them. Then, he cut them open and looked at their internal organs with fascination. Often, he sat on their stomachs as they were dying and laugh. After that, the bodies would be burned in the fireplace, and the ashes thrown away. His last recorded victims were Éonnet de Villeblanche's wife and son, in August 1440.

On May 15, 1440, Gilles kidnapped a priest. The Bishop of Nantes started an investigation. On July 29, he released the findings. The murders of Gilles were uncovered. On September 15, 1440, Gilles was arrested along with two of his body servants, Henriet and Poitou, who were also his accomplices. The charges included sodomy, murder, and heresy. On October 21, Gilles confessed to the charges. On October 23, 1440, the body servants also confessed, and they were both punished with sentences of death. On October 25, Gilles was also given a death sentence. On Wednesday October 26, he was executed by hanging and then burning. The number of his murders is unknown, but it is estimated to be between 80 and 200.

To this day, some question the real guilt of Gilles, stating that he may have been a victim of a conspiracy or act of revenge made by the Catholic Church and French state.

CHAPTER 45: GRAHAM YOUNG

During 1961, the Young family was struck by illness. The four members of the family experienced so much pain and vomiting, and it was discovered that they were suffering from cases of poisoning. The teenage son was the only one with knowledge of chemistry. Some suspected that he may have unintentionally poisoned his family, but no one suspected that the teen was actually experimenting on his victims.

Graham Frederick Young was born on September 7, 1947, in Neasden, North London. His father was Fred Young, and his mother was named Bessie. Three months after his birth, his mother died of tuberculosis. Still an infant, Graham was sent to live with his aunt, while his elder sister, Winifred, was sent to stay with their grandparents. Graham became very close to his aunt and her husband, but when his father remarried in 1950, he was reunited with his family, and his new stepmother Molly. He was very sad to be separated from his aunt, and went on to become a sort of a loner. As soon as he was able to read, he became fascinated with nonfiction murders and Dr. Crippen, who was an infamous poisoner. In his teens, Adolf Hitler fascinated him. He also read about the occult and Wiccans, even involving neighbourhood kids in ceremonies that included sacrificing cats.

At school, he was only interested in chemistry, toxicology, and forensic science, and spent much of his time reading on the subjects. His father bought him a chemistry set to encourage him. When he was only thirteen, he was able to convince local chemists that he was seventeen, and for study purposes, he acquired the poisons antimony, digitalis, and arsenic, as well as the heavy metal thallium. He began his tests by experimenting on Christopher Williams, a fellow science student. Luckily, Christopher survived this experimenting.

In early 1961, Graham started experimenting on his family. He poisoned the tea, and also fell ill himself sometimes, either by accident or to divert suspicion. His sister became quite ill, and in November 1961, it was discovered that she was poisoned by belladonna, but she survived. His stepmother wasn't as lucky. She died the night of April 21, 1962, after going through so much agony. The cause of death was ruled as prolapse of a spinal bone, but she was actually poisoned with thallium after she developed tolerance to antimony. However, since she was cremated, no investigation ever took place. Graham continued to poison his family, bringing his father very close to death. When Graham's school chemistry teacher found various poisons in his desk, he contacted the police. Graham was arrested on May 23, 1962, and he confessed to poisoning his father, sister, and school friend. He wasn't charged with murder of his stepmother since there was no evidence to prove it. However, at the young age of fourteen, he was committed to Broadmoor maximum-security hospital.

Not even imprisonment stopped him. He used cyanide that he extracted from laurel bush leaves to poison fellow inmate John Berridge and cause his death. However, this death was recorded as a suicide. Later, Graham would even poison the drinks of the staff and other inmates. On February 4, 1971, he was declared cured and released from the hospital.

After his release, he started working as a quartermaster at John Hadland Laboratorie. Soon after this, his foreman, Bob Egle, fell ill and died. Graham often made tea with poison for his coworkers, increasing his estimated cases of poisoning to around seventy victims. A few months after Bob's death, another one of Graham's coworkers fell ill and was admitted to the hospital. He suffered for weeks before he died.

At this point, an investigation was necessary. It was Graham who directed the police to consider thallium poisoning, and on November 21, 1971, he was arrested. Antimony, thallium, and aconitine were found in his flat, along with a diary recording on the effects of the poisonings. His trial began on June 19, 1972. He pleaded not guilty, but was convicted and sentenced to life imprisonment. In 1990, Graham died of a heart attack in his cell at Parkhurst Prison.

CHAPTER 46: HAROLD FREDERICK FRED SHIPMAN

Dr. Shipman was a dedicated, hardworking, and loving doctor who wanted nothing but the best for his patients who loved him. They were loyal until death. The unusually high numbers of patients dying under Dr. Shipman's care called for an investigation at last, and it was only then that his secret was revealed.

On January 14, 1946, Harold Fredrick Shipman was born in Nottingham, England. He was the second of four children of Vera and Harold Shipman, a working class couple. Growing up, he was very close to his domineering mother. When she was diagnosed with lung cancer, he voluntarily cared for her as watched her health decline. She had morphine administered at home for the pain in the advanced stages of the disease. Harold was struck by his mother's death on June 21, 1963.

Devastated by his mother's death, he was determined to get into a medical institute and was sent to

Leeds University, a medical school, for training after two years. At age nineteen, he met Primrose, and they soon got married. By 1974, the couple had two children. He began working in Todmorden of Yorkshire, but he was fired for his addiction to painkillers. In 1975, he was admitted to a drug rehab centre. Two years later, Donneybrook Medical Center of Hyde accepted him among the staff.

Soon after, Dr. Shipman's patients began dying at a high rate. Most of those who died were fully dressed and sitting up or reclining on a sofa at the time of their deaths. An alert local office coroner noticed this oddity, and contacted the police. However, the investigation showed nothing incriminating about Dr. Shipman. His history was all in order. It wasn't uncovered until later that Dr. Shipman had been changing his patients' medical history to correlate with the reasons of death that he reported.

It isn't really known when Dr. Shipman began his killings; it is estimated he had as many as 237 victims. He would usually introduce a morphine overdose to the patients. He often targeted lonely and vulnerable elderly women. After their deaths, he would collect the unused drugs for "disposal" and urge the families to cremate the victim. For over twenty years, he went undetected.

His last victim was Kathleen Grundy, a wealthy eighty-one-year-old widow. She was found dead on June 24, 1998. Before she died, Dr. Shipman had visited her, and after her death, he advised the family that post mortem wasn't necessary or required. The victim's daughter, Angela Woodruff, was a lawyer and handled all the legal affairs of her mother. She was shocked to find out that her mother had another will and testament that excluded her children, and left everything to Dr. Shipman. She was convinced Harold had murdered her mother and forged the will to benefit from her death.

Angela Woodruff was determined to find out the truth. She informed the police about her findings, and an investigation was opened. Grundy's body was disinterred, and it was revealed that the real cause of death was overdose of morphine that had been injected within three hours of her death, when Harold was visiting. The police raided Harold's home, where they found medical records for other patients and a typewriter that was used in forging Grundy's will. It was clear then that Dr. Shipman was responsible for more than just one death.

Although many victims were cremated, there were still enough who were buried for the investigation to continue beyond the death of Mrs. Grundy. Police discovered how Harold would digitize medial notes to explain his reasons of the death when the family asked questions. Since the records contained stamped dates, this enabled the police to uncover which records had been changed. Following a thorough investigation, Harold was charged with fifteen murders and one count of forgery on September 7, 1998.

The prosecutors dismissed all the claims that Shipman was acting out of mercy, since none of his patients were actually suffering. Many pieces of evidence contributed to his conviction: the autopsy findings of introduced overdoses of morphine, Angela Woodruff's testimony, fingerprints on Grundy's will showing that she never handled it, the altered computer records, and false prescriptions written to the patients. He was sentenced to fifteen counts of life imprisonment, and four years for forgery, which was later commuted to a whole life sentence. He was imprisoned at Durham Prison. On January 13, 2004, he was discovered hanging by his bed sheets in his own cell.

CHAPTER 47: HARVEY CARIGNAN

All Kathy wanted was a job. On May 1, 1973, she responded to a want ad for employees at a service station. What she didn't know was that she was about to die. Her nude body wasn't found until months later, wrapped up with a sheet of plastic with nickel-sized holes in her skull that had been made with a hammer. It was the work of the man who would later be known as "Harv the Hammer."

On May 18, 1927, Harvey Louis Carignan was born in Fargo, North Dakota. At the time, his twenty-year-old mother was unmarried, but she got married a few years later. At age six, he was small for his size, and suffered from a twitch in his face. He was also a bed-wetter, and had an imaginary friend. At age eight, he was sent to live with his aunt and uncle, but was sent home soon after. At age ten, again he was sent to live with his grandmother, and then with another aunt. At that time, he started stealing. At the age of eleven, he was sent to reform school in Mandan, and was diagnosed with childhood Chorea, a nervous disorder that causes the muscles of the arms, legs, and face to twitch. Harvey claimed that while he was away at reform school, the female employees sexually abused him. At age eighteen, he left the school and enlisted in the U.S. Army.

Harvey started killing in the late 1940s, when he was still in the army. While stationed at Fort Richardson in Anchorage, Alaska, he raped and killed Laura Showatler (age fifty-seven), on July 31, 1949. Almost two months later, he tried to rape Dorcas Callen, but she managed to escape. She reported the incident to the police, and identified Harvey in a line-up. On September 17, 1949, Harvey was brought up to the U.S. Marshal for the murder of Showatler. He confessed, was charged, convicted of first-degree murder, and sentenced to death. However, his death sentence was overturned because the officer who had taken his confession had assured Harvey that he wouldn't be executed, thus violating the McNabb rule. Harvey served eight years in Alcatraz before he was paroled on April 2, 1960.

Between August 1960 and 1968, he was arrested and convicted twice for burglary, assault, and attempted rape, and was imprisoned twice and then paroled. A year after his second release, he married Sheila Moran, a young mother. She divorced him the same year, claiming physical abuse. On April 14, 1972, he married Alice Johnson who had two children. She also left him because of his abuse.

On October 15, 1972, Laura Brock (age nineteen), was found dead due to several blows to the head. On May 1, 1973, after responding to Harvey's ad, Kathy Sue Miller was sexually assaulted and murdered. On

June 28, 1973, Harvey attacked Mary Townsend (age forty-seven) from behind at a bus station. He knocked her unconscious and kidnapped her. In his car, he asked her for sexual favours, but luckily, she was able to escape. Another lucky one was Jerri Billings (age thirteen), who was picked up by Harvey on September 9, 1973. She was assaulted with a hammer and forced to perform sexual acts on him before he released her.

In May 1974, Harvey started dating Eileen Hunley. After she broke up with him, she disappeared on August 10. A few weeks later, her body was found. She had been raped with a tree branch, and then killed with a hammer to her skull. On September 8, 1974, he killed June Lynch (age seventeen) who was hitching rides with Lisa King (age sixteen). Lisa actually escaped.

On September 14, 1974, Harvey picked up Gwen Burton, choked her until she was semi-unconscious, and sexually assaulted her with a hammer. She was dumped and left for dead, but would survive. Four days later, Versoi and Diane Flynn were picked up, but also would survive.

At the time, the police were investigating the matters. Within days, the survivors of the attacks were picking Harvey out of lineups. They all identified him as the man who assaulted them. His possessions were searched, and police uncovered maps marked with 181 red circles (some of them indicating the locations of the attacks).

In February of 1975, Harvey was put on trial for the attempted murder and aggravated sodomy of Gwen Burton. He claimed that God had ordered him to kill those women, and pled not guilty by reason of insanity. The jury didn't believe him and sentenced him to forty years imprisonment. He received other sentences totaling 110 years, but due to Minnesota's law of forty maximum years of imprisonment, he'd never serve them.

CHAPTER 48:
HENRY LEE LUCAS

"Killing someone is just like walking outdoors. If I wanted a victim, I'd go and get one," said the "confession killer" who had claimed responsibility for over 600 murders.

Henry Lee was born on August 23, 1936, Blacksburg, Virginia. His father, Anderson Lucas, was an alcoholic who lost both legs in a workplace accident, and started producing alcohol illegally. His mother, Viola Dixon Lucas, was an alcoholic and a prostitute. Henry had nine older siblings; they all lived in a one-room log cabin. Henry had a harsh childhood. His mother would often abuse him verbally and physically. When he was eight years old, she beat him with a wooden plank on the head, putting him in a coma for three days. On another occasion, when he was given a teddy bear at school, she beat him for accepting it. She would often make him watch her have sex with other men, and made him wear girls' clothes. Once, Henry's uncle gave him a mule that she later killed. When he was ten, he suffered an eye injury during a fight with his brother. Viola ignored the injury for days until it became infected and had to be replaced with a glass eye. He would later be teased and bullied because of it. Henry became alcoholic, and was introduced to bestiality and animal torture.

In 1949, Henry's father died. Henry claimed that when he was fifteen, he kidnapped a seventeen-year-old teenager from a nearby bus stop, beat her until she was unconscious, raped her, and then strangled her to death. In 1952, he was imprisoned with his two half-brothers for burglary. Henry spent one year at an institution for juvenile delinquents. The place was a lot better than the small cabin where he lived. Not long after, in June 1954, he was again sentenced to six years of imprisonment for burglary. He attempted to escape twice but was unsuccessful, and finally was released on September 2, 1959. After that, he moved in with his sister in Tecumseh.

After he moved in with his sister, his mother wanted him to come back home to look after her in her later years. They started to argue and Henry beat her on the neck, causing her to die of a heart attack. Though he claimed self-defense, Henry was sentenced to twenty to forty years in prison after being found guilty of second-degree murder.

In June 1970, he was released from prison due to overcrowding. He then was sentenced to three and a half years of imprisonment for attempted kidnapping. After his release in 1975, he married Betty Crawford, whom he left after she accused him of molesting her daughters. A year later, Henry met Ottis Toole, a sexual deviant working in a soup restaurant in Florida. The two became friends and moved in together in Jacksonville. They both worked at a roofing company from 1979 to 1981. Henry claimed they committed many murders during this period. Henry fell in love with Ottis's then ten-year-old niece, Frieda Powell (she went by Becky because she didn't like her given name). The three of them moved to Texas, and when fifteen-year-old Becky became homesick, she ran away with Henry back to Florida. Ottis became enraged after being left behind and went his own killing spree.

Henry later found a job working for an elderly woman named Kate Rich. On August 24, 1982, he took Becky to a field in Denton, Texas, where he killed and dismembered her body, leaving the pieces scattered in the field. On September 16, he was successful in convincing Kate Rich to come with him to search for Becky. He killed her and dumped her dead body into a drainage pipe. He later retrieved her body and burnt it on a stove.

On June 11, 1983, Henry was arrested for firearm possessions. He was already a suspect in the disappearance of Kate Rich. He confessed and was charged with Kate's and Becky's murders. Police found Kate's bone fragments in the stove, and skeletal remains were discovered in the field where Henry claimed he killed Becky. However, the coroner couldn't positively identify the remains as Kate's or Becky's.

Four days later, he pleaded guilty. Henry continued to confess to numerous murders over the years, but was never convicted of any of them. He was sentenced to death, but his sentence was commuted to life imprisonment. On March 13, 2001, he died in prison from a heart attack.

CHAPTER 49: HIGHWAY OF TEARS

Highway 16 follows the path of British Columbia, Canada. It was given the number 16 in 1942, and is 1,347 kilometres in length. Between 1969 and 2011, along a section of 800 kilometres of the highway, between Prince Rupert and Prince George of British Columbia in Canada, a series of disappearances and murders occurred. To this day, the murders are still unsolved. The official number of eighteen victims has earned Highway 16 the name of Highway of Tears. The actual number of murders is estimated to be much higher, around forty-three.

The first known victim was twenty-six-year-old Gloria Moody. She was last seen on October 25, 1969, leaving a bar in Williams Lake. Her body was discovered ten kilometres away, in the woods at a cattle ranch. In 1970, Micheline Pare (age eighteen) was dropped off by two women on Highway 20, at the gates of Tompkins Ranch, between Fort St. John and Hudson's Hope. She was never seen again.

Two additional murders followed in 1973. Gale

Weys (age nineteen) was hitchhiking from Clearwater to Kamloops in October 1973. Her body was later found in a ditch on Highway 5, south of Clearwater. In November of the same year, Pamela Darlington (age nineteen) was hitchhiking to a local bar when she disappeared in Kamloops. Her body was found the next day.

Another two murders happened the next year. In August of 1974, Colleen MacMillen (age sixteen) left her home in Lac La Hache, hoping to hitchhike to a friend's house nearby. She never made it. She was last seen on 100 Mile House. On December 13, 1974, Monica Ignas (age fifteen) was on her way home from school. She was last seen in Thornhill, British Colombia. On April 6, 1975, her body was found east of Terrace. She had been strangled.

In 1978, Monica Jack (age twelve) disappeared. It wasn't until June 1995, seventeen years later, that some forestry workers found her remains in a ravine off a logging road on Swakum Mountain. Dental records and DNA testing confirmed the remains belonged to Monica Jack. The skeletal remains were found about twenty kilometres from where her bike had been located. In 1996, the police announced they had a suspect, but couldn't lay any charges due to the lack of evidence.

The spree of mysterious killings continued through the 1980s. In 1981, Maureen Mosie (age thirty-three) was last seen in Kamloops. In 1983, Shelly-Ann Bascu (age sixteen) went missing. She was last seen in Hinton, Alberta. Several days later, some of her clothing and blood droplets that matched her blood type were found near the Athabasca River. Her body was never recovered. In 1989, Alberta Williams (age twenty-four) was seen for the last time at Prince Rupert.

In 1990, Delphine Nikal (age sixteen) went missing while hitchhiking eastbound from her place in Telkawa, on Highway 16. On June 11, 1994, Ramona Wilson (age sixteen), was hitchhiking to her friend's home in Smithers. Her remains were found on April 1995, near the Smithers Airport. On a July weekend in 1994, Roxanne Thiara (age fifteen) went missing. She was a prostitute out with a customer, and she was never heard from again. On August 17, 1994, her body was found six kilometres east of Burns Lake. On December 9, 1994, Alishia Germaine (age fifteen) was found stabbed to death behind an elementary school in Prince George. She had stopped working as a prostitute two weeks earlier. Lana Derrick (age nineteen) was last seen at one of the service stations of Thornhill in October 1995.

Nicole Hoar (age twenty-five) was last seen at Prince George in 2002. Tamra Chipman (age twenty-two) was last seen at Prince Rupert when she was hitchhiking to the east on Highway 16 in 2005. Aielah Saric Auger (age fourteen) was murdered in 2006. Loren Donn Lesli (age fifteen) was murdered and Cody Legebokoff (a twenty-one-year-old who was identified later) in 2010. Madison Scott (age twenty) was last seen in Vanderhoof in 2011 after a camping trip.

On September 25, 2012, due to new technologies, a link was found between murderer Bobby Jack Fowler and Colleen MacMillen. Fowler was also a prime suspect in other murders that had occurred on the same stretch of the highway. However, he couldn't have committed the murders of Lana Derrick and the following ones because he was imprisoned from 1996 until his death in 2006.

CHAPTER 50: JACK THE RIPPER

During the late 1880s, horror struck the streets of Whitechapel, London. One gruesome murder after another was discovered and the killer was unknown. More than 125 years later, the mystery surrounding the man who was known as "Jack the Ripper" remains unsolved.

More than a century has passed, and the legend of "Jack the Ripper" is still captivating the minds of the world. The real identity of the murderer and his motives are still unknown. The murderer was dubbed "Jack the Ripper" as a result of a letter published at the time of the attacks, written by someone who claimed to be the killer. Many letters were sent to the London Metropolitan police, to mock them and speculate on more murders. Many theories identifying the killer have emerged: some have named the famous Victorian painter Walter Sickert as the murderer, as well as the grandson of Queen Victoria, and a Polish migrant. Another theory was that a journalist sent the letters to the police to get a scoop, and "Jack the Ripper" is nothing but a mere legend. Unfortunately, the murders did actually occur.

The East End district, where the murders occurred, was a place known for its notoriety, violence, and crime. At that time, prostitution was considered illegal only if it caused public disturbance. Prostitutes were often subject to violence, rape, and even death. Rarely was the death of a "night working girl" ever reported in the press or given attention by the police, but the series of killings that happened in August 1888 were so horrifying that they have gained publicity. A man that obviously hated women committed the murders.

All of the killings took place within a mile of each other, in the districts of Whitechapel, Aldgate, Spitalfields, and London. Although the total number of the murders is still widely debated, it is generally accepted that there were at least five victims. The Ripper had some surgical or medical skills, since all of his victims were mutilated and some of their organs were removed.

His first victim was Mary Ann Nichols (born Walker, age forty-three). She was a prostitute. Mary was found at the entrance of gated stable in Buck's Row (which is now known as Durward Street) on August 31, 1888. Her throat was slit open, exposing the vertebrae. She was also constantly stabbed in the stomach, and her abdomen was cut out and intestines were exposed. She also had two small stabs in her groin area.

His second victim was Annie Chapman (born as Eliza Ann Smith, age forty-seven) who once had sold flowers and liked to crochet, but soon turned to prostitution for fast money. She had contracted tuberculosis and syphilis before the Ripper killed her. She was found on the morning of September 8, 1888, near the entrance of the back yard of 29 Hanbury Street of Whitechapel. She had her throat slashed, and was completely disemboweled. Her intestines were present over her right shoulder, her uterus was missing, and a part of her navel organ as well. What is more horrifying is that murder happened at dawn, in a place close to people who were awake, with only one escape route, yet no one noticed a thing.

Forty-four-year-old Elizabeth Stride (born as Elisabeth Gustafsdotter), also a prostitute, was killed on September 30. She was discovered lying on the ground in Dutfield's Yard (which is now famous as Henriques Street) of Whitechapel, with her throat cut. The killer had also attempted to cut off her ear, but may have been interrupted before he could finish her mutilation.

On the same night, Catherine Kate Eddowes, a casual prostitute like the others, was killed. She was found dead about 1:45 a.m. in a dark and quiet region of the Mitre Square. Her throat was also cut open, and her abdomen was slashed open as well. Her intestines were placed over her right shoulder. Her face was mutilated, and her uterus and left kidney were missing. A package later delivered to the head of the Whitechapel Vigilance Committee with a letter reading "From Hell" contained the missing piece of the kidney.

The last victim was Mary Jeanette Kelly (age twenty-five) who was killed on November 9. She worked in a West End brothel. She was found dead in her room, lying on the bed. Her face was ripped open and her throat was slashed. Her chest and abdomen were cut open and her internal organs were removed. Flesh was engraved from her limbs, and her heart was also missing. She was also pregnant! The killings stopped, but no one knows why. The killer was never found. Many theories still surround the identity of "Jack the Ripper."

CHAPTER 51: JACK UNTERWEGER

Jack was writer. He wrote a novel and an autobiography, and also dabbled in poetry. He was also a murderer who killed prostitutes in his home country and abroad.

Johann "Jack" Unterweger was born on August 16, 1950. His mother was Theresia Unterwegerwas, a waitress and Viennese barmaid. His father was an unknown American warrior. His mother was described as a prostitute by some sources, which would probably explain his hatred towards prostitutes. His mother was arrested many times, and Jack was sent to live with his violent alcoholic grandfather. During his youth, he was often in and out of prison for small crimes and once for assaulting a local sex worker. He was arrested sixteen times between 1966 and 1975, mostly for sexual assault.

He took his first victim in 1974, an eighteen-year-old German girl named Margaret Schäfer. She was strangled with her own bra. In 1976, he was caught, found guilty of murder, and punished with life imprisonment without parole for at least fifteen years. During his time in prison, he became a writer. On May 23, 1990, Jack was released from prison. He later resumed his killings, but his writings had brought him mild fame, and the press and the people of the community advocated him.

His first victim after his release was discovered in Prague on September 15, 1990. Blanka Bockova was found nude and lying on the bed upside down. She was posed with her legs open, and her body was covered with dead leaves. Around her neck, a pair of grey stockings was knotted.

After a few weeks, Brunhilde Masser, a prostitute working in Graz, went missing. In the beginning of December 1990, Heidemarie Hammerer, another prostitute, also went missing. Her body wouldn't be found until a month later, in a wooden place outside the town. She was also found on a bed lying upside down and covered with leaves. She wasn't completely nude, but she was naked from the waist down. A piece of her slip was found in her mouth. She appeared to have been tied up, and then choked with tights. There was evidence that the killer was wearing something red, because red fibers were found on her clothes.

A few days later, the body of Brunhilde Masser, another prostitute, was discovered in the woods in Bregenz, in the same state of the previous victims. On March 7, 1991, Elfriede Schrempf, another prostitute, disappeared. Her skeletal remains were found on October 5, 1991, in a forest outside of Graz. Within a month, four more prostitutes disappeared: Regina Prem, Silvia Zagler, Karin Eroglu, and Sabine Moitzi. The last two were found on May 20, 1992, both strangled with a piece of their own clothes, and dumped in the woods outside Vienna. During this time, Jack was still enjoying his fame, and was working as a reporter while giving his opinion and conducting interviews about the current murders.

August Schenner (age seventy) was a retired investigator who remembered the murders that occurred in the 1970s. They were so similar to the ones happening at that time. The police had already suspected Jack, but they needed to gather enough evidence on this celebrity, as he was known around the community as a "symbol of redemption." They put him under surveillance discreetly, to see if they could tie him to the crimes.

In 1991, Jack went to Los Angeles to work as a journalist. During this time, the murders in Austria stopped, but three prostitutes were murdered in Los Angeles in an identical way to the past murders: Irene Rodriguez, Sherri Ann Long, and Shannon Exley were all beaten, sexually assaulted with branches of trees, and choked with their bras.

The police in Austria were able to link Jack's activities to the place and time of the murders, and there were witnesses who saw him with the victims. In addition, a hair fragment proven to be from Blanka Bockova was found in his BMW. Police were also able to link the murders in L.A. to him. As soon as Jack realized that the police were onto him, he fled the area. He contacted the press in an attempt to look like an innocent victim of the police.

On February 27, 1992, he was found and arrested by the FBI in Miami. He agreed to be extradited back to Austria, where he was eventually found guilty of nine murders. He was sentenced to life imprisonment on June 29, 1994. On the same night, he hanged himself using shoelaces and the same type of knot used on his victims.

CHAPTER 52:
JAVED IQBAL

"You will be strangled to death in front of the parents whose children you killed, your body will then be cut into 100 pieces and put in acid, the same way you killed the children." This was the sentence passed on one of Pakistan's most prolific serial killers.

Javed Iqbal Mughal was born on October 8, 1956, in Lahore, Punjab, Pakistan. Not much is known about his childhood and his life growing up. He was charged twice with sodomy in 1985 and 1990, but he was not convicted of the charges.

During a six-month period, Javed murdered 100 boys. He would lure his victims to his home in Lahore. Most of the boys he lured were beggars and street children between the ages of six and sixteen. After getting them to his home, he sexually assaulted them. Then, he strangled them to death with a chain, dismembered them, and then left the pieces in a vat of hydrochloric acid to dissolve. The remains were then dumped in a local river. Javed kept details about his victims' names and ages, as well as photographs.

In December of 1999, Javed sent a letter to the local police confessing to the murder of 100 boys. The letter was also sent to the new chief editor of a famous

Lahore newspaper called *Khawar Naeem Hashmi*. In the letter, he described details about how he murdered his victims. He claimed that the reason behind these murders was revenge against the police, who allegedly assaulted him one time after arresting him.

His house was searched. Stains of blood were found on the floor and the walls. Police also found the chain he used to strangle his victims. In plastic bags, photographs of his victims were discovered, along with two barrels of acid containing dissolved human remains. Another letter was found in the house, claiming that the remains in the barrels were deliberately not disposed of so the authorities would find them.

In his confession letter, Javed wrote that he wanted to drown himself in the River Ravi. The police started the biggest manhunt known in the history of Pakistan. Nothing was found in the river. Four teenage boys that had been sharing Javed's flat were arrested as his accomplices. Within a few days of the arrest, one of them jumped from a window and died while in the custody of the police.

On December 30, 1999, Javed surrendered by turning himself in at the offices of *Daily Jang*, an Urdu-language newspaper, out of fear that the police might kill him. He was then arrested. Despite all the evidence that incriminated him, such as the detailed diary of the crimes written in his handwriting, he claimed that he was not guilty. He also claimed that the whole confession was a hoax, an attempt to draw attention to the number of children who were running away from their families. He also claimed that he only provided his earlier statements under the pressure from the police.

More than 100 eyewitnesses identified him and

his accomplices and he was given 100 death sentences for his crimes. The judge ordered that he be executed in the similar way he committed the murders, even with the same chain. However, before his execution, Javed was found dead in his prison cell, along with one of his young accomplices who had been convicted along with him. His death was ruled as a suicide.

CHAPTER 53:
JEFFREY DAHMER

aka the Milwaukee Monster

On November 28, 1994, while serving time in prison, Jeffrey Dahmer was assigned to work with fellow inmates and convicted murderers Jesse Anderson and Christopher Scarver. They were left alone for twenty minutes to complete their tasks, and when the guards returned, they found that Christopher had killed the other two by beating them to death. The events that led Jeffrey to his fate started many years before.

Jeffery Lionel Dahmer was born on May 21, 1960. His parents were Joyce Annette, a Teletype machine instructor, and Lionel Herbert Dahmer, a student at Marquette University who later graduated as a chemist. His mother was always seeking attention of his father who was mostly away. His parents often quarreled, and Jeffrey was neglected.

At school, he was known as a quiet kid with a small group of friends. From a very early age, Jeffrey was interested in animals, especially dead ones. He collected dragonflies, butterflies, and insects to put them inside jars. He also collected dead animals from the side of the road, and dismembered them for his collection. After his father's graduation, the family moved to Ohio. Jeffrey became an alcoholic during his adolescence, even drinking at school. During puberty, he realized that he was gay. He often fantasized about being completely dominant over his partner. He graduated in May 1978 at the age of eighteen. His parents got a divorce, and his mother won custody over his younger brother. He was legally an adult.

In June 1978, he picked up a man named Steve Hicks, who was hitchhiking to a rock concert. He invited him home where they drank and had sex. When Steve tried to leave, Jeffrey struck him in the head with a barbell, killing him. He then dismembered the body, placing the parts in plastic bags and burying them in the woods.

In January 1979, Jeffrey dropped out of university due to his uncontrolled drunkenness, and under his father's urging, he enlisted in the Army. He was later discharged due to alcoholism. In October 1981, he was sent to live with his grandmother in Wisconsin. Five years later, he was arrested for masturbating in front of two boys.

His second murder occurred in September 1987. He met Steven Toumi at a gay bar, they went to a hotel room, got drunk, and Jeffrey killed him. He then took him back to his grandmother's basement, sexually assaulted him postmortem, dismembered the body, and disposed of it.

For the next four years, he murdered fifteen gay African-American men in total. He met them mostly at gay bars, invited them to his grandmother's basement where they would drink until they passed out.

Then, Jeffrey strangled his victims, and either engaged in necrophilia to assure his control over the victim, or masturbated on the body. He dismembered the corpses and disposed of them. Sometimes, he kept their skulls or genitals. At different stages of the murders, he also took photos so he could later relive the experience of every step of killing his victim, and masturbate in front of the skulls that he collected.

He was once charged with the sexual assault of a thirteen-year-old Laotian boy. He pleaded guilty and claimed that he thought the boy was older. While waiting for his trial, he claimed another victim, Anthony Sears, an aspiring African American model, in February 1989. He was tried three months later. He was sentenced to one year in prison on day release, and five years of probation. After his release, he rented his own apartment in May of 1990.

During the next fifteen months, he killed twelve more. He continued his rituals, and began experimenting with chemicals in order to dispose of the bodies. He also engaged in cannibalism, consuming his victims' flesh. In addition, while they were still alive, he would try to drill into their skulls, attempting to complete a lobotomy. His victims died instantly. He carefully selected men whose disappearances wouldn't be much noticed.

On July 22, 1991, two policemen picked up Tracy Edwards. He claimed that he had been drugged and restrained by Jeffrey. Upon entering the apartment, the officer noticed the gruesome pictures. He informed his colleague, who was successful in restraining Jeffrey after a fight. Further searching revealed the human "trophies" that Jeffrey kept.

The trial began on January 13, 1992, under very strict security due to the racist nature of the attacks. Jeffrey confessed to the murders but pleaded not guilty by reason of insanity. On February 17, 1992, he was found guilty and sentenced to fifteen consecutive life terms. He was killed in prison in 1994.

CHAPTER 54: JERRY BRUDOS

It was almost the end of January 1968. Linda Salwson was going door to door, trying to sell sets of encyclopedias. She was only nineteen years old, trying to work her way to college. She went to a neighbourhood in Portland, Oregon. She would never be seen again, and no clues were left to what had happened to her. Only her abandoned car was found.

Born on January 31, 1939, Jerome Henry Brudos had two other older brothers. His parents moved to many different homes before settling in Oregon. After having two boys, his mother had been hoping for a girl. She didn't want him and often abused him, belittling and criticizing him. Growing up, he developed a sexual fetish for women's high heels shoes and underclothing.

When he was five years old, he found a pair of spike-heeled shoes in the trash, and took them. When his mother saw him wearing them in the bedroom, she took them away, destroyed them, and yelled at him. Her reaction probably made him think that these women shoes were something deliciously forbidden, and he became more attached to them. He later stole the shoes of his kindergarten teacher. When he was seventeen, he kidnapped and beat up a young woman, threatening her with a knife. Jerry was arrested and taken to a psychiatric ward. He was evaluated and diagnosed with schizophrenia. His sexual fantasies fed his hatred toward his mother and women in general. In 1957, he graduated from high school, and later became an electronics technician.

In 1961, he married his seventeen-year-old girlfriend. Together, they had two children. He continued to steal women's shoes and underwear, and later started murdering women.

Jerry Brudos is considered to be one of the cruelest criminals of his time, as he did not pay mercy to anybody. His first murder was of Linda Salwson, although he was never convicted of it since her body was never found. On November 26, 1968, twenty-three-year-old Jan Whitney was on her way home when a mechanical failure in her car forced her to hitchhike. She disappeared.

On March 27, 1969, Karen Sprinker (age nineteen) was supposed to meet her mother for lunch. Her mother waited and waited, but Karen never showed up. Her car was parked at the garage where she had planned on meeting her mother, but there was no sign of Karen. One month after Karen's disappearance, Linda Salee (age twenty-two) was kidnapped from a shopping mall where she was trying to buy a gift for her boyfriend. Her car was also found, but police could find no signs of violence.

Jerry sexually abused his victims post mortem. He also dressed them up in clothes of his choosing, and took photographs of them. He sometimes kept trophies of his victims. He dressed them up in high heels and masturbated after the murders.

Three weeks after the disappearance of Linda, a man fishing in the Long Tom River found a body. The body was of a female, tied up to a car transmission box so that the body would sink in the water. The knot and the copper wire were twisted in a way that showed that the killer was someone with the knowledge and skills of an electrician. At the opposite sides of the rib cage, a needle apparently caused two postmortem punctures circled by a burn.

Dental records confirmed the remains were of Linda Salee. Through further searching, Karen Sprinker's body was also discovered in the river. She was tied to an engine head with the same type of knots found on Linda Salee. Karen appeared to have been strangled, and her breasts were missing.

The police interviewed students from the Oregon State University, who described a strange man around the campus, leading them to Jerry Brudos. Jerry confessed to the murders under questioning. He was charged with the murders of Whitney, Sprinker, and Salee and was sentenced to three consecutive terms of life imprisonment. On March 28, 2006, Jerry died in prison from liver cancer.

CHAPTER 55:
JOE BALL

Joe Ball was known as the "Butcher of Elmendorf," the "Bluebeard of South Texas," and the "Alligator Man." Although not much is known about what happened during his life, the Joe Ball story still lives. It is a legend that would go on for generations.

Joseph D. Ball was born on January 7, 1896. He was the second of eight children to Frank and Elizabeth Ball. Growing up, he didn't like to participate in many activities with other children. Instead, he usually spent his time fishing and exploring. In his teen years, he became passionate about guns, spending many hours each week practicing how to shoot and perfecting his skill. His father became very rich and owned many properties.

When the U.S. declared war on Germany in 1917, Joe enlisted in the army and served in Europe. In 1919, he was honourably discharged, and went back to his hometown, Elmendorf. For a while after, Joe worked for his father. During the Prohibition, he worked as a bootlegger, delivering illegal whiskey and beer. He hired Clifton Wheeler, a young African American man, to help him. After the Prohibition, Joe opened his own saloon, The Sociable Inn.

Two bedrooms were located in the back of the inn, and a bar in the front. He dug a hole behind the bar, cemented it, filled it with water, and then put five alligators in it. This attraction brought in many customers who enjoyed watching the alligators eat live animals (mostly cats and dogs).

Joe always hired the best looking waitresses. This attracted more customers. Being a player, he often got involved with them, until one day, he decided to get rid of some of them.

The employees at Joe's began to mysteriously disappear. The first to go missing was Minnie Gotthardt or 'Big Minnie' as she was known, and Hazel 'Schatzie' Brown vanished next. Joe was questioned many times, especially when Minnie's family wanted to know her whereabouts, but he maintained his innocence. A few months after dismissing Joe as a suspect in the disappearances, another family began looking for their twenty-three-year-old daughter, Julia Turner, who worked part time at The Sociable Inn. Again, Joe was questioned, and he claimed that Julia had some problems with her roommate, and he had lent her money to help her move on. However, employees kept on disappearing.

On September 23, 1938, a neighbour of Joe's went to the police claiming that he saw Joe feed his alligators human remains. Another person claimed that there was a barrel left by Joe at his sister's that smelled like something dead was in it. The next day, deputies John Gray and John Klevenhagen went to investigate. The barrel was gone. Again, they went to question Joe, and when they told him that he would be taken to San Antonio for more questioning, he grabbed a .45 caliber revolver and shot himself. (Some sources claim he shot himself in the heart, and some in the head, nevertheless, it was fatal.)

The investigation led the deputies to discover rotting meat, and an axe with blood and hair on it. To get more answers, Bexar County Deputy Sheriff decided to question Clifton Wheeler, the person who would have likely helped Joe. Wheeler proved to be of help. He confessed that he had helped Joe in hiding two bodies. He led the police to the remains of Hazel Brown, near the San Antonio River. Her body was decapitated. He claimed that Joe killed her because she fell in love with another man and wanted to run away with him. The head was burned in a campfire near the discovered body. As for Minnie Gotthardt, Wheeler claimed that Joe had killed her because she became pregnant, and he didn't want to ruin his relationship with his wife, Dolores. Joe took her to an isolated area and shot her after a night of drinking. On October 14, 1938, her decomposed body was found. Wheeler was questioned about other disappearances, but claimed he only knew about these two murders. He was sentenced to two years in prison, and after serving them, he left the town and disappeared because he couldn't start a life there.

Until today, Joe Ball's exact number of victims is still unknown. It is also not known if he really fed human remains to his alligators.

CHAPTER 56: JOHN CRAWFORD

In the early 1990s, a series of murders targeting Native American women in Canada occurred. It is believed that the murders committed by John Crawford went largely unnoticed because the victims were all Aboriginal women. It is a case that focuses on the uncaring society towards marginalized minorities.

On March 29, 1962, John Martin Crawford was born in Steinback, Manitoba. He was the eldest of three children. At the time of his birth, his mother wasn't married, but she later got married. He had a stepbrother and a stepsister younger than him. His stepfather was reported to be an alcoholic, and worked as a taxi driver. When he was just three years old, John started trying to run away from home. His babysitter molested him when he was four and again when he was seven. In 1966, John suffered from burns on his upper chest, neck, and arm when he was playing with a cigarette lighter; he was later bullied because of the scars. When failing the first grade at the age of five, teachers told him that he was stupid. At the age of twelve, he started to sniff glue and take prescription drugs. He also began drinking. He had his first sexual encounter at the age of thirteen, with two males and an eleven-year-old girl that they paid to have sex with. When he was sixteen, John claimed that he started hearing voices in his head that would torment him.

On December 23, 1981, John committed his first murder. At the age of nineteen, he murdered thirty-five-year-old Mary Jane Serloin in Saskatchewan, Canada. John was arrested, and found guilty of manslaughter. He was sentenced to spend ten years in prison. While imprisoned, he was evaluated by a psychiatrist after trying to mutilate himself. John was released from prison in 1989, when he met his later partner, Bill Corrigan. The series of murders would continue in 1992. Between 1989 and 1992, John was often accused of raping and abusing prostitutes by beating and choking them.

All of his later murders took place in Saskatchewan, Canada. His second victim was Shelley Napope, a sixteen-year-old girl. She was beaten and stabbed to death. This was the only murder that Bill Corrigan helped him. Another victim was Eva Taysup. She was strangled to death on September 20, 1992. The last victim was murdered the next day. Calinda Waterhen was strangled to death on September 21, 1992. The remains of his victims wouldn't be found until 1994. John raped his victims and mutilated them. He would also move his victims so they would be very difficult to find. Shelley was hidden at the scene. Eva and Calinda were moved and buried. Before burying Eva, John sawed off her arm.

In January 1995, John was arrested for the murders of Shelley, Eva, and Calinda. His trial began on May 21, 1996. He was convicted of second-degree murder for Calinda and Eva, and first-degree murder for Shelley. He was sentenced to three counts of life imprisonment at Saskatchewan Penitentiary in Prince Albert. In 1999, John tried to appeal his sentence, but he was denied. Currently, he is still serving his three concurrent life sentences.

CHAPTER 57:
JOHN GACY

It was "Pogo the Clown"! John dressed up like a clown, "Pogo the clown," a character that he invented to entertain children. He was known to be actively involved in charity work. Everyone in the community regarded him as a charming person, someone who always tried to make things better. Nobody knew that he was also the reason behind making things so much worse, and deadly...

John Wayne Gacy, Jr. was born on March 17, 1942. He was the second child of a middle class Irish Catholic family. He was the middle child, and had two sisters. At the age of eleven, he suffered from a blow on his head while playing, which led to him having blackouts for the next five years. His father was an alcoholic and homophobic. Growing up, he was always the subject of his father's verbal and physical abuse. Although his father constantly beat him up, John still worshiped him, and continued to long for his approval.

After dropping out of high school, John enrolled in a business school. There, he excelled and after his graduation, he landed a job as a management trainee at a footwear company. During this time, he became involved in many community organizations. He would even dress up as a clown to entertain children.

In September 1964, John married coworker Marlynn Myers and the couple moved to Iowa. He started working as a manager to three Kentucky Fried Chicken restaurants, and also volunteered to work with the Jaycees, an organization for the community. With Marlynn, he had two children, Michael (born in March 1967) and Christine (born in October 1968). During that time, there were rumours that John had made sexual advances towards many teenage employees. John was charged with sodomizing Mark Miller, a young employee, in May 1968. He claimed that he was innocent. However, after four months, he hired Dwight Anderson, another young employee, to beat up Mark and stop him from testifying. Dwight was arrested, and he confessed to being hired by John. John was convicted and sentenced to ten years in prison. His wife and children left him, and he never saw them again. His father died while he was serving his time.

Being a model inmate, John only served eighteen months, and was paroled on June 18, 1970. He agreed to return to Chicago to live with his mother, who bought him a ranch style house. There he managed to keep his criminal record from his neighbours, and was again a good participator in the wellness of the community. On June 1, 1972, he married Carole Hofgen, who already had two children.

In 1974, John started his own business, PDM Contractors. He hired many teenage employees, a business tactic that provided him with his victims. His neighbours often complained about the smell coming from his house, which he attributed to the moisture buildup under his home.

Between January 3, 1972 and December 11, 1978, John murdered thirty-three boys. He would sometimes kill more than one boy on the same day. His first victim was fifteen-year-old Timothy Jack McCoy. He would lure the young men to his house, with a promise of discussing a job or doing magic tricks with handcuffs. Once his victim was handcuffed for the "trick," he would overpower him. Only his first victim was stabbed; the other ones were strangled or gagged with their underwear. Before killing them, he would drug them, then torture and rape them. Some of his victims were gay prostitutes, but most of them were PDM employees.

In May 1978, Jeffrey Ringall was lured into John's car. John drugged his victim, then raped and tortured him. For an unknown reason, he didn't kill him. Jeffrey reported the incident to the police, and charged John with sexual assault.

In late 1978, fifteen-year-old Robert Piest disappeared. The police were alarmed and looked into John's history of sexual conviction. They searched his house on December 13, 1978, where they found driving licenses and college rings that helped link John to the victims. The search of the space under his house led to the discovery of twenty-seven bodies. On December 22, John confessed to the murders of more than thirty people, and led the police to where he had disposed of the remaining victims.

On February 6, 1980, John was charged for thirty-three murders. He was found guilty, and was sentenced to death on March 13, 1980. He would wait fourteen years in prison for his execution. On May 10, 1994, John was executed by lethal injection.

CHAPTER 58: JOHN PAUL KNOWLES

Lester was good looking and charming. As a compassionate and caring man, he knew his way around women. So, it was no surprise when Sandy, a British journalist, became "enchanted" by him. However, Sandy still had a weird feeling when it came to Lester, who told her that he wanted to "leave a mark on life...to be remembered for something," and soon she would discover the awful secrets that he was hiding.

Paul John Knowles was born on April 17, 1946, in Orlando, Florida. When he was only eight, he became involved in petty theft, so his father put him in a reformatory foster home. During his years growing up, he had his share of run-ins with authorities, mostly for burglary. When he was nineteen, he kidnapped a policeman after he was stopped for traffic violation, and was arrested and imprisoned. From that time on, he spent almost half of his remaining living years in prison. He tried to go straight in 1970 after meeting a woman, but he gave it up after finding the straight life hard.

In 1974, he was serving some time in a Florida prison when he started writing to Angela Covic, a divorcee living in San Francisco. Their relationship progressed, and when she came to visit him, he proposed and she accepted. With the help of her lawyer friend, she helped him get out of prison. As soon as he was released, he flew to California to meet with her. However, a clairvoyant had recently warned Angela about a dangerous person in her life, which she interpreted to be Paul, and she broke up with him.

Paul later claimed that after Angela broke up with him, he allegedly killed three people, but this could never be verified. He was eventually arrested after a bar fight and was imprisoned again, but he was able to escape on July 26, 1974. His killing spree had started.

Hours after his escape, he broke into the home of sixty-five-year-old Alice Curtis. He tied her up and gagged her. Paul went on searching her home for something valuable to steal. Alice choked and died at some point, but it isn't known if she died while Paul was still present or after he left. He also stole her car. While driving, he recognized Lillian (age eleven) and Mylette (age seven) Anderson, two family acquaintances. He was afraid they might identify him, so he kidnapped and strangled them. He later dumped their dead bodies in a swamp. On August 1, he kidnapped a young girl, thirteen-year-old Ima Jean Sanders, and killed her. She wouldn't be identified until 2011.

On August 2, 1974, Paul met Marjorie Howie (age forty-nine). He strangled her in her apartment with a nylon stocking. On August 23, he went into the house of Kathie Sue Pierce, and with her three-year-old son present, he strangled her with the telephone cord that he cut. He didn't harm her son. On September 3, he met thirty-two-year-old William Bates in a pub near

Ohio. He strangled him, dumped him in the woods, and stole his car. On September 18, he shot Lois and Emmett Johnson, two elderly campers, and stole their credit card. A few days later, he met Charlynn Hicks in Seguin, Texas. He kidnapped her, raped her, and strangled her with her pantyhose. He went on to kill ten more people. He stole a tape recorder, which he used to record a confession from one of his victims, and arranged a secret meeting with his lawyer to give him the tape. After killing Carswell Carr along with his daughter (age fifteen), he met a reporter named Sandy Fawkes and spent several days with her using a fake name. Sandy had a close experience with him, not knowing that he was a wanted serial killer; he didn't kill her.

On November 17, a Florida highway patrol trooper named Charles Eugene Campbell identified Paul and tried to arrest him alone. He wasn't successful, and ended up getting shot dead, along with another civilian, James Meyer (the last victim). Later, Paul tried to crash through a roadblock of police, but he hit a tree. He took off on foot, and after a chase, he was apprehended.

Paul ultimately claimed the responsibility for thirty murders, but only eighteen could be attributed to him. He gave a detailed confession of his killing spree. On December 18, Paul took Agent Ronnie Angel of Georgia Bureau of Investigation and Sheriff Earl Lee to the place where he dumped State Trooper Campbell's handgun. He was able to free himself from his handcuffs using a paperclip, and tried to grab the sheriff's gun. However, Agent Angel shot him three times in the chest, killing him instantly.

CHAPTER 59: JOHN STRAFFEN

"What would you do if I killed you? I have done it before." The thirteen-year-old girl trembled under the threat. The young man had his hand covering her mouth. The girl was lucky—the man left her unharmed, and she was able to report the incident to the police. She knew the man's name was John, but the police wouldn't connect the dots until much later.

John Thomas Straffen was born on February 27, 1930, in Borden, Hampshire. He was the third child in his family. His father was a soldier. When he was two years old, his father was sent abroad, and the family spent the next few years in India. It wasn't until the year 1938 that the family returned to England and settled in Bath.

John was a quiet kid at school, affectionate but a loner. When he was eight years old, he started committing thefts and was skipping classes, so he was referred to a Child Guidance Clinic. In 1939, he stole the purse of a girl and was given two years of probation. His probation officer noticed that he didn't really know the difference between right or wrong. At the age of ten, with an IQ much below average (his IQ was 58, while the average is 100), he was sent to St Joseph's School in

Sambourne, a school for mentally defective children. He wouldn't be released until he was sixteen.

A year later, the incident with the thirteen-year-old girl happened. That year, he also strangled five chickens, and was sent to another colony to handle his situation in Almondsbury, north of Bristol. It was revealed that he was mentally disabled, possibly due to an encephalitis attack from when he lived in India, which may have caused a brain damage. However, he was still released.

On July 15, 1951, John was walking around. On his route, he met five-year-old Brenda Goddard, who was gathering flowers not far from her foster parents' home. He offered to show her a better place to pick up flowers. He walked her into the woods nearby, where he strangled her. John didn't try to hide the body; instead, he left her there and continued his walk like nothing happened. John was a suspect in the police's investigation, but he wasn't considered violent, and was dismissed.

On August 8, 1951, another girl would meet John's death grip. Cicely Batstone (age nine) was seeing a movie, "Tarzan and The Jungle Queen," at the cinema. John was there, and he struck up a conversation, promising her to take her to another cinema to see "She Wore a Yellow Ribbon." They got on the bus, and John took her to a nearby field and strangled her, making her his second victim. This time, however, there were witnesses. The bus driver and the wife of a policeman both saw them together. The wife of the policeman even told her husband because she thought that it was odd.

After the disappearance of Cicely, John was immediately considered to be a suspect. With the help of the witnesses, the police arrested him. John confessed to the murder of Cicely, and also to the murder of Brenda before even being asked. On October 17, 1951, John stood for trial, but was found to be unfit by reason of insanity. He was committed to the Ministry of Health institution, and was given a job as a cleaner.

On April 29, 1952, at 2:40 p.m., John escaped the hospital by jumping over the wall, evading the guards in the process. He was captured four hours later, seven miles away. At 10:30 p.m., Linda Bowyer (age five) was reported missing. She was last seen riding her bicycle around the village a few hours earlier. John was immediately suspected, and after his recapture, the police went to his room even before the news about the murder had gotten to the hospital. When asked if he had done anything at the time of his escape, he immediately stated, "I did not kill her." When he was told that a girl was found dead near where he escaped, he said, "I did not kill the little girl on the bicycle." John was charged with the murder of Linda, and this time found to be sane. He was sentenced to death, which was later commuted to life imprisonment. On November 19, 2007, he died in prison, after serving a record fifty-five years in prison, the longest sentence in British history.

CHAPTER 60: JUAN VALLEJO CORONA

Juan Corona was just a Mexican who wanted to live and work in the U.S. during the 1950s. No one could have known that such a simple man would turn out to be one of the most prolific serial killers at that time.

Juan Vallejo Corona was born in 1934 in the Jalisco state of Mexico. In 1950, when he was just sixteen years old, he entered the U.S. illegally by crossing the borders to California. After three months of picking carrots and melons in the Imperial Valley, he moved to Sacramento Valley. In May 1953, he joined his brother, Natividad Corona, who had already migrated to the country in 1944. They settled in Marysville, Yuba City. Juan got married in 1953 for the first time, and then in 1959, he married Gloria Moreno, with whom he had four daughters.

In December 1955, a massive flood caused a wide destruction in the area where they lived, and thirty-eight people were killed. After going through this experience and seeing all the deaths that surrounded him, Juan had a mental breakdown. He also suffered from schizophrenic episodes. On January 17, 1956, his brother committed him to the DeWitt State Hospital, where he was diagnosed with schizophrenia and paranoia. After receiving twenty-three shock treatments over the next three months, he was released and declared cured. He was then deported back to Mexico, until he acquired a green card and came back to the states legally. He was a hard worker, but still experienced schizophrenic episodes and a violent temper. In 1962, after becoming a licensed labour contractor, he started hiring workers for the local fruit ranches.

Juan did not approve of gay men, even though his brother was gay. Natividad owned a café, the Guadalajara Cafe in Marysville. On February 25, a customer named Jose Romero Raya was attacked with a machete in the café's bathroom. Natividad reported the incident to the police and Jose filed a lawsuit against him, which forced Natividad to sell everything and flee to Mexico instead of paying the $250,000 judgment. In March 1970, Juan was committed to the hospital again.

Juan had killed over twenty-five men and buried them in the ranches he was working for. He would kill them by strangulation, stabbing, or he would shoot them. When the bodies were discovered, some were badly decomposed, and some were still freshly buried. Most of his victims were discovered in a bunkhouse on the Sullivan Ranch.

Most of the evidence gathered against Juan was circumstantial. For example, in one grave, meat receipts with Juan's signature were discovered. In other graves, deposit slips from Bank of America with his name and address were found. Moreover, many witnesses testified that Juan was last seen with the victims on many occasions, usually in his pickup truck.

On May 26, 1971, the police obtained a search warrant, and entered Juan's house to arrest him. His wife and daughters were so surprised. More evidence was discovered at the house. The police found two knives with bloodstains on them, a machete (like the one used in Raya's attack), a pistol, and clothing with bloodstains on them. The police also found a work ledger with thirty-four names and dates. Seven victims were included in that list. The list was the most important evidence against Juan.

Juan initially entered a plea of not guilty by the reason of insanity. The search for the victims ended on June 4, and a total of twenty-five victims (all white males) were found. Four of the victims couldn't be identified. This suggested that more victims had not been found.

On July 12, Juan was indicted for twenty-five murders. His trial didn't start until a year after the discovery of the bodies. On September 11, 1972, the trial began. On January 18, 1973, Juan was found guilty for the twenty-five murders, and was sentenced to twenty-five terms of life imprisonment. During his time in prison, he suffered from heart problems, and was once in a stabbing incident.

In January 1974, his wife filed for divorce, which he granted on July 30. On May 18, 1978, his conviction was overturned, and he was tried again on February 22, 1982. Seven months later, he was convicted of the crimes again. Currently he is serving his time in the Security Housing Unit (SHU), and won't be eligible for a hearing again until 2016.

CHAPTER 61:
KARL DENKE

A few days before Christmas Eve, on December 21, 1924, while everyone was happily going about their holiday business, Vincenz Olivier was fighting for his life. He was barely able to escape his attacker. Covered in blood, he showed up at the police station and reported the attack that almost took his life. However, Olivier was a vagrant, and he was accusing a very decent citizen. Nevertheless, the police were obliged to investigate after the doctor who was giving medical care to Olivier confirmed that he was really wounded.

Karl Denke was born in what is now known as Ziębice, Poland, on August 12, 1870. Not much is known about his early life. It is reported that he wasn't very good at school, and at the age of twelve, he ran away from home. His family was a wealthy family of farmers. After his graduation from elementary school, he began an apprenticeship under a gardener. At age twenty-five, he started a life on his own. After his father's death, his older brother took over the farm. He bought a piece of land with the money that he inherited, but farming didn't go well, so he sold it. He bought a little house, but due to the inflation in the country at that time, he was forced to sell it. He eventually settled into a little apartment on the ground floor of a house. Karl was so well liked in the community that he soon began carrying the cross at Evangelist funerals, and also played the organ at the church during services. He was also called "Papa" because he was known to be affectionate.

No one would suspect the true dangerous and evil nature of Karl. He killed his first victim in 1909, twenty-five-year-old Emma Sander. Not much is known about his later victims, but it is estimated that he killed at least thirty persons. He would lure his victims to his apartment. Usually, they were beggars, tramps, or anyone who wouldn't be missed around the neighbourhood. There was no evidence of sexual assault, and his motives were not completely clear. He would kill with an axe, and dispose of his victims' flesh by selling it as pork. He would pickle the flesh in jars, and sell it in the market.

It all came to an end on December 21, 1924, when Olivier reported Karl Denke to the police. At first, the police didn't believe him. But when he wouldn't change his story, they were obliged to arrest him. Karl claimed that he had hit Olivier when the beggar tried to steal from him. However, the police kept Karl in prison for more investigation. That same night, Karl was found dead in his cell. He was so desperate to commit suicide that he used a handkerchief to hang himself.

The police searched his apartment and they found all the evidence of the horrible things that he did. There were twelve different identification papers for various travelers, clothing, two drums with large pieces of meat in brine, many types of bones, and pots full of fat as well.

The reason behind the awful things that Karl did will never be known. He took his secret to the grave with him.

CHAPTER 62:
KARLA HOMOLKA

Karla was caught in the mix of love, evil, and insanity. No one would be safe from her sick soul, not even her sister. As an accomplice to her fiancé and then husband, she is considered to be one of the most infamous serial killers.

Karla Leanne Homolka was born on May 4, 1970, in Port Credit, Ontario. Her parents were Dorothy and Karel Homolka. She was the oldest of two other sisters, Lori (born 1971) and Tammy (born 1975). Growing up, Karla was pretty and popular, and loved by her family and friends. She loved animals, and after her high school graduation, started working at a veterinary clinic.

When she was seventeen, Karla attended a convention in Toronto. There, she met Paul Bernardo, a twenty-three-year-old man, who was smart and charming. On the day they met, they had sex. The two started a relationship. Later, they would both discover that they had the same sadomasochistic desires. Karla became obsessed with fulfilling Paul's fantasies.

Over the years, both Paul and Karla kept feeding their psychotic behaviour. Paul became involved in raping women, while Karla knew about it and approved. The police, who were searching for him, had dubbed him the Scarborough Rapist. He attacked women as they got off the bus, raped them violently, and humiliated them.

In time, Paul became attracted to Karla's little sister, Tammy. He always complained about how Karla wasn't a virgin when they first got together. Karla decided that she would help her fiancé rape her little sister as a gift to him. She stole Halothane, an animal anesthetic, from her work place. On December 23, 1990, at a Christmas party at her family's home, Karla and Paul drugged Tammy. They took her to the basement after the rest of the family went to sleep. Karla put a piece of cloth containing Halothane on Tammy's mouth to keep her unconscious. During the rape, Tammy choked on her own vomit and died, without ever regaining consciousness. Before calling the police, the couple hid any evidence of the assault. Tammy's death was ruled as an accident and no drugs were detected in her system.

After that, Karla and Paul moved in together. In an attempt to replace Tammy as a sexual object for Paul's sick enjoyment, Karla invited a teenager to dinner, intoxicated her, and gave her to Paul. The couple spent the whole night raping her violently, but she managed to survive when she woke up the next day, not knowing what had happened.

On June 15, Paul kidnapped Leslie Mahaffy. Again, the couple raped her for many days, and videotaped some of the assaults. They later killed her, dismembered her body, put the pieces in cement, and dumped the cement in a lake. Her remains wouldn't be found for two weeks.

On June 29, the couple got married. A few months later, on April 16, 1992, they kidnapped Kristen French (age fifteen) from a church parking lot. They brought her home, tortured her, and raped her, all while still videotaping their acts. She was still alive until the couple decided to spend the Easter Sunday dinner with Karla's family. They killed Kristen then. Her body wouldn't be found until April 30.

In January 1993, Paul's physical abuse caused Karla to leave him. During that time, the police were still working on the capture of the Scarborough Rapist. They had successfully identified Paul as the rapist, and captured him. Karla was questioned as a person of interest. With the walls closing in on her, Karla confessed to all their brutal actions together, obtained a lawyer, and started working on her plea bargain. She portrayed herself as one of Paul's victims. In the end, the prosecutors struck a "deal with the devil," giving her twelve years in prison in exchange for her testimony against Paul. Further evidence of the videotapes made it clear that she was so much more involved in the crimes, but nothing could be done by that point.

On July 4, 2005, Karla was released from prison. Harsh restrictions were placed on her release: she was required to give the police her home and work address, and the name of the person she lived with. She was also required to notify them of any changes to this information or any changes to her name. If she wanted to be away from home for more than forty-eight hours, she was required to give seventy-two hours' notice. She was also forbidden to contact Paul, the family of the victims, or any violent criminal, to be alone with people under the age of sixteen, and to take drugs other than prescription medicine. She also agreed to continue therapy and counseling and to give authorities a DNA sample.

She lived in Quebec for a while, where she married and gave birth to a son. It is reported the couple is currently living in Guadeloupe with their three children.

CHAPTER 63: KENDALL FRANCOIS

Kendall Francois was the youngest in his family. He lived with his parents and sister. He told his parents that a family of raccoons died in the attic, and that was the source of the smell. He was having a hard time removing the carcasses. Nobody knew his dark hidden secret.

Kendall Francois was born on July 26, 1971, in Poughkeepsie, New York. He went to Arlington High School where he played on the football team until his graduation in 1989. One year later, he joined the Army. For his basic training, he went to Fort Still, Oklahoma. In 1993, he went to the Dutchess County Community College where he took classes in liberal arts. He was a student, on and off, for five years, until 1998. Between 1996 and 1997, he worked as a school monitor in the Arlington Middle School. While he had a clean record in the school, his behaviour turned inappropriate with some of the female students. He would often touch their hair and tell them sexual jokes.

Kendall kidnapped his victims, beat them, and

then killed them. During the years between October 1996 and August 1998, women began disappearing from the town of Poughkeepsie. All the missing women were white, slim, with a small build, and had brown hair. They all disappeared around the same area near Kendall's home. The victims were: Wendy Meyers (age thirty, disappeared in October 1996), Gina Barone (age twenty-nine, disappeared in December 1996), Kathleen Hurley (age forty-seven, disappeared in January 1997), Catherine Marsh (last seen alive on November 11, 1996, though she wasn't reported missing until March 1997), Mary Healy Giaccone (missing in November 1997), Sandra Jean French (age fifty-one, disappeared on June 12, 1998), and Catina Newmaster (disappeared in August 1998). There was no crime scene, so no profile could be established for the abductor. However, since all the disappearances were happening around the area where Kendall Francois lived, and because he was reported to be very rough during sex by local prostitutes, his home was placed under surveillance.

On September 1, 1998, a kidnapped prostitute was able to run away from Kendall's home after freeing herself from his grip. Kendall had been strangling her. Later that same day, two detectives investigating the disappearance of Catina Newmaster were handing out flyers in the area. They stopped at a gas station, and there, a woman named Deborah Lownsade reported to them that another woman, the prostitute, had just left claiming that she had been assaulted. The detectives went after the woman, and she confirmed the attack. At the police station, the prostitute filed a complaint against Kendall. The police immediately went to talk with Kendall, and asked him to come down to the police department. Under questioning over the next several hours, Kendall admitted to his involvement in the disappearance of the women. He was arrested on the spot.

On September 2, after obtaining a search warrant, investigators went to search Kendall's house at 99 Fulton Avenue. There, they made the gruesome discovery of the bodies of the women, Kendall's unfortunate victims.

Two days later, Kendall was charged with the murder of Catina Newmaster. On September 9, he pleaded not guilty in court. On October 13, due to the evidence at his home, he was charged with eight counts of first- and second-degree murders, and one count of attempted murder. On December 23, Kendall changed his plea to guilty in order to avoid the death penalty.

On February 11, the court refused to accept his guilty plea, but when it was discovered that Kendall Francois had contracted HIV from one of his victims, the case was taken to the State Court of Appeals, and the guilty plea was upheld. On August 11, 2000, Kendall Francois was sentenced to life imprisonment without the possibility of parole. Currently, he is serving his sentence in the Attica Correctional Facility.

CHAPTER 64:
KENNETH BIANCHI

The women trusted these two policemen. They would go with these men wherever they asked. After all, they were police officers. What the women didn't know is that it was all fake. Under the false badges of these officers were serial killers.

Kenneth Alessio Buanchi was born on May 22, 1951, in Rochester of New York. His mother was only seventeen, and she was an alcoholic prostitute. She gave him up for adoption soon after his birth. Frances Sciolono and Nicholas Bianchi became his adoptive parents. Growing up, Kenneth liked to lie. He also had trouble sleeping and would often wet his bed.

Although he had an amazing IQ, he always did poorly in school. His mother, Frances, decided to send him to a private elementary school to set him straight, but he didn't do much better. In 1964, his father died, causing his mother to pull him out of the private school and enlist him in a public school. There, he dated often and also joined a biking club. After his graduation in 1971, Kenneth married his girlfriend from high school, but they divorced eight months later due to the couple's immaturity. He wanted to be a police officer, and after unsuccessful attempts, he joined a security company. He was always looking for the easy way out of a situation, so he started stealing from his employees, forcing him to keep moving from one job to another.

In 1975, Kenneth moved in with Angelo Buono, his cousin seventeen years his senior, in California. At work, Kenneth met Kelli Boyd and moved in with her, and in May of 1977, she became pregnant.

Kenneth began a series of murders with his cousin on October 18, 1977. Their first dupe was nineteen-year-old Yolanda Washington, whom they beat, raped, and strangled with a piece of fabric. They dumped her body near the entrance of Forest Lawn Cemetery, leaving her in a strange pose. Their third victim was Judith Ann Miller (age fifteen) who was found strangled and positioned in a diamond shape on October 31, 1977. On November 6, Elissa Kastin (age twenty-one) was found beaten, raped, strangled, and dumped naked close to Kenneth's house. On November 9, Jill Barcomb (age eighteen) was found in the same manner in the north of Beverly Hills. Unfortunately, because the victims were all prostitutes and runaways, these murders didn't garner much attention from the community.

On November 18, high school student Kathleen Robinson (age seventeen) was found dead. Two days later, Dolores Cepeda (age twelve) and Sonja Johnson (age fourteen) were also found dead. These three vulnerable young victims were found raped, sodomized, strangled, and disposed of at different hillside areas, thus the killer (as it was then believed to be only one person) was dubbed "The Hillside Strangler." On the same day, November 20, Kristina Weckler was found at another site; she had been brutally killed by being injected with cleaning fluid. The police interviewed Kenneth because he lived in the same apartment complex as the victim, but he wasn't considered as a suspect. The torture techniques seemed as if they were being refined after each murder.

More victims were claimed: Jane King (age twenty-eight), Lauren Wagner (age eighteen), Kimberly Martin (age twenty-two), and later Cindy Lee Hudspeth (age twenty-three). During this time, Kenneth had been driving along with the police in search of the killer (he was still pursuing his dream to work in the law enforcement). When Angelo found out, he forced Kenneth to escape to Bellingham in Washington, and be with Kelli and their son. There, he joined a security company and started as a security guard, and claimed his last victims.

On January 11, 1970, he lured two higher education students, Diane Wilder (age twenty-seven) and Karen Mandic (age twenty-two) to a house he was guarding. He raped, strangled, and dumped them in Mandic's car. However, without his partner, he left many clues. The police were able to connect him to the murders and arrest him. After many unsuccessful tries to escape prosecution, such as claiming insanity and schizophrenia, Kenneth finally confessed and agreed to testify against his cousin.

While in prison, he charmed a female admirer, Veronica Compton, enough to convince commit a copycat murder in hopes he would be proven innocent, but she got caught. In 1983, Kenneth was sentenced to life imprisonment, which he is still serving to this day in Washington State Penitentiary. He won't be eligible for parole until the year 2025.

Kenneth is also suspected to be involved in the Alphabet Murders, which occurred during the early 1970s, but there's no evidence enough to be sure.

CHAPTER 65:
KENNETH ERSKINE

Elderly people are often considered to be the weakest humans. They usually aren't able to defend themselves. It was those people that merciless Kenneth preyed upon.

Kenneth Erskine was born in July 1963. His mother, Margaret, was British and his father, Charles, was Antiguan. His parents abandoned him at a young age. At the age of twenty-four, he was diagnosed as having the "mental age of eleven." Not much is known about his early life, but there were reports of him trying to hang his younger brother John twice. More reports indicate that he started using drugs at the age of sixteen, and when he tried to give cannabis to John, his parents kicked him out and disowned him. He spent the next seven years of his life homeless, drifting through the streets of London. He was involved in burglary and theft, until at one time he had ten different bank accounts for his stolen money. He was a loner with no friends and a violent temper. He also preyed on elderly people.

In 1986, he leveled up in his crime career from burglary to murder, and was able to take the lives of at least seven elderly people. He would break into their homes, usually from an unattended window since there was no forced entry, attack them, strangle them, and sometimes sexually assault them, although the sexual abuse couldn't be determined if it happened before or after death. It appeared that Kenneth knelt on his victims' chests, and put his left hand on their mouths and his right hand on their throats to strangle them to death. Out of his seven victims, four of them were sodomized.

He claimed his first victim on April 9, 1986. It was Eileen Emms, a seventy-eight-year-old woman. It wasn't until police realized that a television set was missing from her flat that her death was considered to have been a murder. A postmortem made it clear that she had been raped and strangled. Two months later, on June 9, Janet Cockett (age sixty-seven) was found dead. This time, Kenneth's palm print was left on the scene; it was found on a window in the victim's flat.

On June 28, at a residential home in Stockwell, two Polish pensioners and WWII veterans were found dead after being sexually assaulted and strangled. They were Valentine Gleim (age eighty-four) and Zbigniew Strabawa (age ninety-four). The fifth victim was found dead on July 8 of the same year. William Carmen (age eighty-two) was sexually molested and then strangled to death. Kenneth also stole money from his victim before killing him. A few days later, on July 21, 1986, William Downs (age seventy-four) was also killed in the same manner.

Kenneth claimed his final victim two days later, on July 23. Florence Tisdall (age eighty-three) was a widow living in a retirement complex in Fulham. Her caretaker found her dead. After killing his victims, Kenneth often put them back in bed to make it look as if they died during sleep. Because of this, it is possible the total number of his victims is actually much higher.

On July 28, 1986, Kenneth was arrested. He went with the police without a fight. Investigators had identified his palm print as being left at the scene of Janet Cockett's murder. A surviving victim of one of his attacks also identified him: Frederick Prentice (age seventy-four), whom he had attempted to strangle on June 27.

Kenneth claimed that he heard a woman's whispers telling him to commit these murders, and that he didn't really remember killing. He was finally charged with seven murders, and one attempted murder; two murders were eliminated for insufficient evidence. He was convicted on January 29, 1988, and sentenced to seven counts of life imprisonment and twelve additional years for the attempted murder charge, with the recommendation that he wouldn't be considered for parole before the forty-year minimum. In July 2009, Kenneth appealed, and the conviction was reduced to manslaughter on the grounds of diminished responsibility.

CHAPTER 66:
KRISTEN GILBERT

"If my patient in ICU dies, can I get off early?" asked Nurse Kristen Gilbert. The answer was yes, and within hours, the patient died from cardiac arrest.

Kristen Heather Gilbert was born on November 13, 1967, as Kristen Heather Strickland. Her parents were Richard and Claudia Strickland, and she had a younger sister. She lived in a happy family, more or less, without any significant problems. She grew up to be pretty and smart, but she was also a chronic liar. She was so natural in lying that it became hard to differentiate between truth and lies. She would also steal from her friends, and was later described as "strange and controlling." To get attention from her boyfriends, she would fake suicide, and sometimes get so angry she would attack them.

In 1988, Kristen became a registered nurse and married Glenn Gilbert, with whom she had two children. Her coworkers saw her as committed to her job and very social. She had high skills as a nurse, and reacted well under pressure during emergencies. However, under her care, an angel of death was in hiding.

After giving birth to her first baby in 1990 and coming back to work, things changed for Kristen. During her shifts, the mortality rate tripled, but she was still admired by her coworkers for her skills. After the birth of her second child in 1993, her marriage began to deteriorate, and she began an affair with James G. Perrault, a VA Hospital security guard. In 1994, she left her husband and children for her lover. During that time, the deaths on her shift were increasing, and whispers of suspicion filled the hospital's halls. Patients with no history of heart problems were suddenly dying of heart attacks. Epinephrine went missing.

On February 2, 1996, she killed her patient in the ICU so could get off her shift early. Kristen would administer epinephrine to her patients so they would go into cardiac arrest. Then, her boyfriend, James, would be called to the ICU. There, she will be able to impress him with her skills, get close to him, and flirt with him.

On February 15, she flushed the intravenous lines of an AIDS patient getting treated with antibiotics. At that time, nurses reported their suspicions. Federal investigators almost immediately linked the deaths to Kristen. She worked for seven years at the VA hospital, where 350 patients died under her watch. The number was too high to be all attributed to coincidence. It is speculated that she was responsible for at least eighty murders, and over 300 emergencies.

When the investigation began, Kristen was not present. In her absence, the death rate dropped dramatically. When she started to appear as guilty, James began to pull away from her, ending the relationship in June of 1996. On July 8, she took an overdose of drugs, and was admitted to a psychiatric ward. During her stay, she confessed the murders to James who informed the federal grand jury, and he later testified against her.

In an act of revenge, and an attempt to delay the investigation, she phoned the hospital pretending to be a man and claimed that three bombs were to go off in two hours in Building One. Patients and staff were evacuated. This resulted in her arrest and conviction, and she would spend fifteen months in a federal prison. The exhumation of the bodies that Kristen was responsible for killing had started at that time. In 1998, Kristen was charged with four murders and three attempted murders by epinephrine injection. On March 14, 2001, she was found guilty of three counts of first-degree murder, one count of second-degree murder, and two counts of attempted murder. She was sentenced to life imprisonment without the chance of parole for at least twenty years.

CHAPTER 67: LAWRENCE BITTAKER

"Are you going to kill me?" the girl asked. "No," replied Roy with an evil look in his eyes. The girl knew her fate; she had accepted it. "Before you do, give only one second, to pray."

Lawrence Sigmund Bittaker was born on September 27, 1940. His birth mother put him in an orphanage where he was adopted by George Bittaker and his wife. George worked in the aircraft factories, which is why the family had to move often, and Lawrence grew up in four different states. When he was only twelve, Lawrence started his criminal career by committing petty thefts and shoplifting. He was arrested many times. Although he had an IQ as high as 138, he dropped out of high school in 1957. He was in and out of prison until 1974.

His first attempted murder was in 1974. He stabbed a supermarket clerk, Gary Louie, next to his heart when he questioned him about an object he was stealing. Gary survived. Lawrence was convicted and imprisoned in California's Men Colony. It was there that he met Roy Norris in 1977, and they became friends. Together, they would fantasize about kidnapping, raping, and murdering teenage girls.

After getting out of prison, Lawrence met up with Roy, and they started planning for their killing spree. They purchased a van for their kidnappings, and in June 1979, they started picking up female hitchhikers to develop a method to lure their victims. They also discovered a secluded area where they could kill.

On June 24, 1979, Lawrence and Roy picked up their first victim. Lucinda Lynn Schaeffer (age sixteen) was dragged into the van. She struggled but they were able to bind her. They took her to their chosen location and raped her, one after the other. Despite the circumstances, she didn't shed any tears, as if she knew what would happen. She only asked to pray before getting killed, a request which was denied. In the end, Lawrence strangled her, and they wrapped her with a plastic shower curtain and threw the body over a canyon, leaving her for the animals.

On July 8, they picked up Andrea Hall (age eighteen) as she was hitchhiking to visit her boyfriend. Hiding in the back of the van, Roy grabbed her and subdued her. He gagged Andrea and was able to bind her wrists and her ankles. They took her to their secluded area, and raped her. Lawrence liked to humiliate his victims even more by making them perform oral sex on him, taking pictures of them, and make them beg for their lives. He then thrust an ice pick into both of her ears, piercing her brain. While still conscious, he strangled her, and dumped the body over a cliff.

On September 3, Jackie Gilliam (age fifteen) and Jacqueline Leah Lamp (age thirteen) were taken into the "death van." Jacqueline tried to escape, but was unsuccessful. They raped her multiple times, took pornographic pictures of her, and Lawrence even tape-recorded himself raping her. After two days of being held hostages, the victims were killed. Jackie was stabbed in each ear with an ice pick, and then was strangled. Jacqueline was hit on her head with a sledgehammer, strangled, and then bludgeoned.

The final victim, Shirley Lynette Ledford (age sixteen), was kidnapped on October 31, 1979. She was tortured, raped, and sodomized by the pair for about two hours in the van. They even made recordings of the torture. In the end, Roy strangled her with a coat hanger. They then dumped the body on a lawn chosen randomly, where it was discovered the next day.

The reason for their arrest would initially be because Roy liked to brag. He told an old inmate and friend, Jimmy Dalton, about the crimes. Jimmy told his attorney, and he was advised to tell the authorities, which he did. Details given to Jimmy matched details of rapes committed by the pair. A woman, Robin Robeck, who was raped by the men but released, was able to identify them as the rapists.

The two were put under surveillance, where police learned that they were also dealing marijuana. On November 20, 1979, they were both arrested. A search of their apartments turned up incriminating evidence. Ten days later, and under duress, Roy confessed. In February 1980, they were both charged with five murders. On March 24, 1981, Lawrence was sentenced to death. He appealed several times. Currently, he is still on death row.

CHAPTER 68: LEE BOYD MALVO

"Dearest police, Call me God ... Your children are not safe." The shootings were getting worse. The whole state was terrorized. People were afraid to even leave their homes.

Lee Boyd Malvo was born on February 18, 1985, in Kingston, Jamaica. He spent his childhood in Jamaica with his father, Leslie Samuel Malvo, who was often absent, and his mother, Una James, who was constantly leaving him unsupervised with others. In 1998, he moved with his mother to Antigua. There, he met John Allen Muhammad (born Williams) who became like a father figure to Lee. In 2001, Lee and his mother moved to the U.S. using false documents. They lived in Miami, and then moved to Washington. Lee's mother then moved back to Florida and left Lee with John, who was very controlling. John claimed that he was Lee's stepfather, and got him into high school. Lee didn't make any friends there. Lee stole a .223 semi-automatic Bushmaster XM-15, and practiced shooting with John in a firing range.

John and Lee started their sniper shootings in the fall of 2002. In Maryland and Louisiana, they shot four people, killing three of them and injuring one.

After a month, they started shooting people in Washington, D.C. The community lived in fear during this time. Everyone was afraid to leave their home, pump gas, or even cross a parking lot, since multiple victims were shot doing simple everyday tasks such as this.

They killed their victims with the rifle that Lee had stolen. They chose their victims randomly, with various ages and sexes. The victims were killed with one shot. They fired from the trunk of their car, which they prepared with an aiming hole above the license plate. The shots were fired from 50 to 100 yards away. At many of the crime scenes, they left tarot cards. Once they left the Death card, with the words "Call me God" on the front. Some of the other cards they left read: "Code: Call me God," "Do not release to the press," and "For you Mr. Police." Once, they left a ransom note. They demanded ten million dollars from the government in order to stop the shootings. According to Lee, John told him that they would use the money to train a completely black community somewhere in Canada, so they could commit acts of terrorism all over the states. Before the Beltway shootings, John and Lee used other guns to attack victims. In the Metropolitan area in D.C. only, they killed ten persons and injured three. They had about seventeen victims in other places.

Since there was no pattern in choosing the victims, the police faced much difficulty in determining the killers. After the last shooting, the police received an anonymous phone call advising them to look into a robbery – a homicide that had happened in Montgomery, Alabama. Suddenly, there was a break in the case. At that scene, there was a fingerprint left by Lee.

On October 4, 2002, the police found Lee and

John sleeping in their car. They arrested them. Shell casings found in the place where they practiced their shooting matched those extracted from the victims.

Since the sniper shootings took place in different states, they were tried separately in those states. Lee claimed that John was the one in charge during the shootings, and that he killed the first six victims. In an interview in 2012, Lee also claimed that John had sexually abused him. In December 2003, Lee was found guilty of the murder of FBI analyst Linda Franklin in Virginia. His sentence was life in prison without the possibility of parole. In 2004, he pled guilty for one murder and one attempted murder in Virginia, and he received two more life sentences. In 2009, in Maryland, Lee was again sentenced to six counts of life imprisonment for the six murders committed there. Currently, Lee Boyd Malvo is still serving his sentences in the maximum-security facility at the Red Onion State Prison of Virginia.

CHAPTER 69: LUIS ALFREDO GARAVITO

It was June 8, 1996. It was still early afternoon when a young boy from Boyaca went missing. His mother started searching for him immediately. It was reported that the boy was hanging out with other boys at a local shops. A strange man had bought the group some sweets and then left. Some five days later, the boy's body was found. He had been decapitated and his severed penis was stuck in his mouth. "The Beast" had struck again.

Luis Alfredo Garavito was born on January 25, 1957, in Génova, Quindío, Colombia. He had seven younger brothers. Not much is known about his childhood, other than that his father often abused him physically and emotionally. Later, Luis was also a victim of sexual abuse; two of his male neighbours raped him repeatedly. After only five years in school, Luis dropped out and left home at the age of sixteen. He started working as a store clerk, and then selling prayer cards and religious icons as well. His adult life didn't get any better. He was an alcoholic who kept on changing jobs.

He was also aggressive and kept moving from one town to the other. At least once, Luis attempted to commit suicide.

Luis's victims were chosen from poor families. They were also street children. They were mostly between the ages of eight and thirteen, with one victim aged sixteen. Luis would get close to the children and gain their trust by buying them sweets or asking them to help him with odd jobs. He would also take them for long walks, and when they became tired, he tied them to a tree. Then, he would torture them, rape them, sodomize them, and kill them by cutting their throats. He killed more than 140 boys all over Colombia, and maybe in Ecuador when he travelled there.

On April 22, 1999, a homeless man saw a male trying to abuse a twelve-year-old boy, hiding in the bushes. The man was apprehended, and he gave the name and identification of a small town politician. At that time, there was no file network to check people out. The man, Luis, was put in the prison, because he matched the description given. A year earlier, some corpses of boys were found. Since there was no possibility for DNA checking, the cases were left open.

With the evidence closing in on him, Luis confessed to the murder of 140 children. He gave details of his murders and their locations. He claimed that he had committed the murders when he was drunk. Luis was charged and found guilty of 139 murders. However, since Colombian law has a maximum sentence of thirty years, he would not receive a life sentence or the death penalty. Moreover, his sentence was reduced to twenty-two years because he was cooperative in helping the police in finding the victims. He is still under investigation, as more murders are uncovered. The law has been criticized as Luis's release comes closer. A judicial review of his cases found that his sentence could be extended when he will have to answer for his crimes that were not covered by the earlier judicial progress.

CHAPTER 70: MARCEL FELIX PETIOT

Smoke poured out of the chimney from the home at 21 Rue le Sueur, Paris. The neighbours became suspicious. The smoke had been going on for days, and the smell was unbearable. No one was in the house. Dr. Petiot, the owner, was away. After about five days, the neighbours complained to the police. The police came in to investigate, and what they discovered was terrifying.

On January 17, 1897, Marcel Andre Henri Felix Petiot was born in Auxerre, France. He had one brother, Maurice. Many accounts were kept about his childhood, but it is not known if they were facts or mere tales. It is said that he enjoyed torturing animals. He was intelligent, but a loner. From an early age, he was known for his inappropriate behaviour and theft. He would also have convulsions, was a bed-wetter, and would sleepwalk. He was constantly being expelled from schools. On March 26, 1914, he was diagnosed as mentally ill.

In January 1916, he joined the French army. He witnessed battles, and continued stealing. He was again diagnosed as mentally ill, and was discharged towards the end of 1918. After that, through a special accelerated education program made for war veterans, Marcel was able to receive a medical degree in eight months. He started working, and soon was supplying narcotics to addicts.

In 1926, Marcel was involved in an affair with Louise Delaveau who was the daughter of one of his elderly patients. Soon, Louise disappeared. This was supposedly his first murder. He continued his life of embezzlement as the elected mayor. In 1932, after many complaints about his thefts, he fled to Paris. There, he had fake credentials, and was able to attract many patients. He performed illegal abortions, and was still giving prescriptions to drug addicts.

His main income came from his murders. As a ruse, he let people think that he could provide them with an "escape route." There were many people who were wanted by the Germans, such as Jews, criminals, or resistance fighters. He used the name "Dr. Eugène." He claimed that he could give them false identities and help them escape towards Argentina or anywhere in South America, through Portugal. He would do that in return for 25,000 francs for each person. He had three accomplices, Edmond Pintard, René-Gustave Nézondet, and Raoul Fourrier, who would help him by directing victims his way. Once the victims provided Marcel with the money, he convinced them that they needed to be vaccinated. Under his control, he injected his victims with cyanide, killing them almost instantly. He would then steal their valuables and dump the bodies. To get rid of the bodies, he threw them into the fire and let them burn.

Around 1941, the Gestapo heard about that "escape route" that he was providing, and launched an investigation to capture him. They thought that this plan was a part of the Resistance. Through an informer, the Gestapo was able to find Marcel's accomplices, torture them, and imprison them. They revealed the identity of "Dr. Eugène," however, Marcel was nowhere to be found.

On March 11, 1944, after neighbours complained about the smoke coming out of his house and the police investigated, human remains were found in the basement. During the next seven months, Marcel went into hiding and took another identity. It wasn't until October 31 that Marcel was arrested. He was imprisoned, but claimed that he only killed enemies of France and he was innocent. He claimed that he worked with the Resistance, but there was no proof to this. Some of the Resistance groups that he claimed he worked with never even existed. He was charged with at least twenty-seven murders, and his motive was pure profit. He was tried on March 19, 1946. The jurors did not believe his claims that he was a hero and convicted him of all twenty-six murders. He was sentenced to death. On May 25 of the same year, Marcel was executed by beheading.

CHAPTER 71: MICHAEL BRUCE ROSS

In May of 1981, a body was found in Ithaca, New York. It was later identified as the twenty-five-year-old Dzung Ngoc Tu. At first, it was believed that she had committed suicide. However, later it was discovered that actually she had suffered a violent rape and had been murdered. This was only the beginning.

Michael Bruce Ross was born in Connecticut on July 26, 1959, as the eldest of Dan Graeme Ross and Patricia Hilda Laine. His parents' marriage had been in trouble since the beginning. His mother became pregnant in high school, and was forced to marry his father. Patricia often abused her children (Michael had two younger brothers and a younger sister), and saved the worst for Michael. She constantly beat him up. She had a history of mental illness, was admitted twice to a mental hospital, and even left home once. It was also suggested that eight-year-old Michael was sexually molested by his young uncle who committed suicide at the age of fourteen.

Although Michael had a dysfunctional childhood, he still excelled in school. He was interested in animals. In 1977, he graduated high school and in 1981, he graduated university with an agriculture degree. At school, he was very social, but all his relationships with girls were doomed with failure. After starting college, he had started having violent sexual fantasies, and began stalking women in his second year. Later, he began raping the women he stalked.

His first murder was of Dzung Ngoc Tu, mentioned earlier. He claimed his second victim on January 5, 1982. He kidnaped seventeen-year-old Tammy Williams. Not far from the place where she disappeared, she was found raped and strangled to death. About two months later, Michael picked up Paula Perrera who was hitchhiking to her boyfriend's house. She was also raped and strangled to death.

On April 2, 1982, he tried to attack a pregnant off-duty policewoman at her house. She struggled and he wasn't successful, and instead was arrested. However, he made bail, and was sent to Connecticut for psychiatric evaluation. He was free to continue his killings.

On June 15, 1982, Deborah Taylor (age twenty-three) was walking on the road looking for a gas station as her husband looked for one in the other direction. Michael kidnapped her, and then raped and strangled her. Four months later, her skeletal remains were found. Michael was still not suspected. In 1982, Michael pled guilty for the assault of the policewoman, served four months in jail, and was later let out on probation.

He went back to Connecticut, and on November 19, 1983, he kidnaped Robin Stavinsky (age nineteen), raped her, and strangled her to death. Her remains were found a week later. A murder pattern was visible to the police investigating, and they were able to link this death to the other victims. On Easter Sunday of 1984, Michael kidnapped Leslie Shelley and April Brunais (both fourteen years old) while they were walking home. They were both brutally raped. He again strangled his victims to death.

His eighth and final victim was Wendy Baribeault (age seventeen), who was murdered on June 13, 1984. She was also raped and strangled. However, this time, there witnesses who claimed seeing a "thin white man with glasses driving a blue late model Toyota" following Wendy on the same day that she disappeared.

There were 3,600 Toyotas that matched the description given by the witnesses in the area. The detective visited the first person on his list, which was Michael, on June 28, 1984. The detective was immediately suspicious of Michael. In the end, Michael couldn't keep quiet anymore, and confessed to the murders. His trial began in July 1987. He was convicted of all the murders. In total, he was sentenced to two counts of life imprisonments, and six death sentences.

After many appeals, and much fighting to evade the death penalty, Michael accepted his fate and decided to stop appealing. On May 13, 2005, he was executed by lethal injection.

CHAPTER 72: NANNY DOSS

"Until death do us part"... and death came too soon...

Nancy Hazel was born on November 4, 1905. She had three sisters and one brother. Her mother, Loulisa, was caring, but her father, James, was violent. Her family was poor. She received little education since she was forced to stay at home and help her father in the farm most of the time. Growing up, he father forbade her from going out, having friends, wearing make-up, and dressing up in nice clothes. To fuel her romance fantasies, she often read romance magazines. She was always searching for her ultimate romantic experience all her life. She was nicknamed Nanny.

It was reported that when she was seven, the family went on a train trip. When the train stopped suddenly, Nancy hit her head on a metal bar, and as a result, suffered from headaches and blackouts for the rest of her life. She would later blame her future criminal actions on this incident.

At age sixteen, she met Charley Braggs and married him after just four months. Charley was an only son, and they lived with his mother. Between 1923 and 1927, they had four daughters. The pressure of taking care of her family and having to put up with her mother-in-law led to her drinking and smoking heavily. Her husband began cheating on her, and she on him too. At that time, two of their daughters (the middle ones) died of food poisoning. Charley suspected that Nanny had killed them, so he left her and took his eldest daughter with him. Not long after, he returned with the divorce papers in the arms of another woman.

After that, Nanny went back to her romance magazines, the lonely hearts column especially, and started writing to men. In doing so, she met Robert "Frank" Franklin (age twenty-three), who was a factory worker. In 1929, they married, and remained so for sixteen years. She later found out that he was an alcoholic, and also had a criminal record.

She lived with him and her two daughters. During that time, her eldest daughter got married, and in 1943, gave birth to a baby boy named Robert. Two years later, she gave birth to another baby who died soon after. On July 7, 1945, two-year-old Robert mysteriously died from asphyxia while in the care of Nanny. She would later collect the insurance money. In 1945, after a night of heavy drinking, Frank forced sex on Nanny. She put rat poison in his whiskey jar, and he died a painful death the same day.

Nanny again went back to search for romance in the lonely hearts column. She met Arlie Lanning, and married him only after three days. However, she soon discovered that he was no better than Frank; he was alcoholic and a womanizer. Nanny would leave from home for months, but would always return playing the role of a housewife. Arlie soon died, and soon after his funeral, the house left for his sister burned down, and Nannie collected the insurance money. Her mother-in-law mysteriously died in her sleep.

Nanny moved in with her sister who also died soon after. At that time, she joined the Diamond Circle Club to look for a husband. There, she met Richard L. Morton, another womanizer. In January, Nanny's mother came to live with them, and soon, she too was poisoned to death. In April 1953, Richard was also poisoned and died.

Nanny didn't waste any time, and soon found husband number five. In June 1953, she married Samuel Doss. He was a good man, but he disapproved of Nanny's romance readings. Three months later, Samuel went to the hospital with a digestive infection. He was released back home, in Nanny's care, on October 5. The same evening, Samuel died.

The death of Samuel made his doctor suspicious, so he ordered an autopsy. It was revealed that his system contained a significant amount of arsenic. Nanny Doss was then arrested. She confessed to all the murders. She was found mentally fit for the trial, and on May 17, 1955, after pleading guilty, she received life in prison. She was only charged with the death of Samuel Doss. In 1965, while serving her life sentence in the Oklahoma State Penitentiary, Nanny Doss died of leukemia.

CHAPTER 73: OTTIS TOOLE

Adam's head was found on July 27, 1981. The rest of his body was never recovered. Adam was only six years old. He was a cute little boy and his death was a tragedy that devastated the Walsh family.

Ottis Elwood Toole was born on March 5, 1947, in Jacksonville, Florida. His father was alcoholic and he abandoned his family. His mother was abusive, and often dressed him up in girls' clothes. As a child, Ottis was sexually abused by his older sister, his next-door neighbour, and other relatives and friends. Ottis was also mentally challenged, with a below average IQ of 75. He also suffered from seizures due to epilepsy. He often ran away from home, and slept in abandoned homes. He also was an arsonist, and discovered that fire aroused him sexually.

He dropped out of school, and began frequenting gay bars. He became obsessed with watching gay pornography. Apart from being a beggar, he also worked as a male prostitute to support himself.

Ottis committed his first murder when he was only fourteen. After a traveling salesman propositioned him for sex, he ran over him with the salesman's own car. In 1974, he was a prime suspect in the murder of Patricia Webb (age twenty-four) in Nebraska, so he fled to Colorado. There, he was again a prime suspect in another murder committed on October 14, 1974. The victim was Ellen Holman (age thirty-one). Again, Ottis left, and came back to Jacksonville. In 1976, he married a woman in an attempt to hide his homosexuality, but when she discovered the truth, she left him.

In 1976, at a soup kitchen, Ottis met Henry Lee Lucas, and they started a relationship. Henry would be Ottis's partner in murder too. Their murders went undetected for years. In April 1983, Ottis was arrested on a charge of arson. After two months, Henry was also arrested for firearm possession. Henry started boasting about their crimes. Ottis first denied his involvement, but later confessed.

Ottis confessed to the murder of Joana Holter (age forty-six), whom he killed with a machete. He also confessed to setting the house of George Sonnenberg (age sixty-four) on fire while he was still in it, which killed him. He also strangled and killed Silvia Rogers (age nineteen). He was also guilty of six unsolved murders, four in Jacksonville and two in Florida. He confessed to the shooting murder of a nineteen-year-old hitchhiker named David Schallart. He also killed Ada Johnson (age twenty) by shooting her in the head.

In April 1984, Ottis was sentenced to death for the murder of George Sonnenberg. He received another death sentence for the murder of Silvia Rogers. Both sentences were commuted to life imprisonment. He also received life sentences for his confessions of the unsolved murders. Ottis claimed that he helped Henry murder 108 victims, but that was never verified.

Ottis also confessed to the murder of Adam

Walsh, though he later retracted his confession. He did this twice. There was not enough evidence to convict for this murder, especially since the police mishandled some of the evidence. In 2008, it was officially announced by the police that Ottis was the one who murdered Adam. His niece told the police that on his deathbed, Ottis confessed to the murder of Adam.

On September 15, 1996, Ottis died of liver failure in his prison cell. He was forty-nine years old. Since no one claimed his body, he was buried in the prison cemetery. The exact number of his victims is still unknown.

CHAPTER 74: PATRICK KEARNEY

On March 17, 1977, seventeen-year-old John Malay did not come home after going out to meet with a guy. His mother called the police, who dismissed the case as a runaway. Five days later, his remains were found. He had been dismembered. Parts of his body had been drained of blood and packed in sealed trash bags. His head was missing, but police were able to identify his remains due to a birthmark.

Patrick Wayne Kearney was born on September 24, 1939. He had two older brothers. As a child, he was thin and shy, and would often get sick. He was constantly bullied in school. Growing up, he had detailed fantasies about murdering people.

He got married briefly, and then divorced. Patrick was gay, and would frequent gay bars in San Diego and Tijuana looking for potential partners. In public, he seemed normal, but a monster was lying within. In the year 1962, Patrick met David Douglas Hill near Los Angeles. It was love at first sight. David was married, but soon got divorced and moved in with Patrick who got a job working as an aeronautics engineer. They spent ten years together, but fought so often that David left and returned many times. During this time, Patrick would blow off his feelings of frustration and anger by killing.

During the times they fought, Patrick would take long solitary drives in his car. He would then pick up young men who were hitchhiking or out at gay bars. Patrick didn't have a large build, so he shot his victims in the head with his .22 caliber pistol to subdue them. He steered the car with his left hand while shooting his victim with his right hand. He was careful not to go over the speed limit and attract unwanted attention. Then, he would keep his victim in the passenger seat until he found a good place to do whatever he wanted. Once a suitable place was found where he could be alone with the body, he undressed it, and then practiced necrophilia. Sometimes, after finishing, he would beat the corpse repeatedly as if to let out his rage. After that, he used a hacksaw to dismember the victim and cut it into pieces. If he was in his home, he performed his ritual in the bathroom, and washed each part of the body. This drained it of blood, got rid of any smell, and washed away any fingerprints or dry blood. Some victims looked like the guys who used to bully him at school. However, Patrick never tortured his victims while they were alive.

The murder of John Malay was probably the last murder committed by Patrick. However, this time, John had told his neighbour that he was going to meet a guy named Dave in Redondo Beach. The police soon went looking for David and Patrick. The couple allowed the police to collect carpet fibers from their home. These fibers matched those found on the tape sealing the bags of John's remains. The police came back and took hair samples from the couple and their dog. Again, the evidence matched. However, when the police came back a third time for the arrest, Patrick and David were gone. The police then found a hacksaw with blood and tissue from the victim left on it, residual blood of victims all over the bathroom, and the same filament tape and trash bags that had been used to hide the parts of the victims. Photographs of Patrick and David were distributed so that the public would be able to recognize the killers.

On July 1, 1977, the couple surrendered themselves to the sheriff's office. Patrick confessed to the murders. He claimed that he took the life of his first victim in 1968. He gave full details of his crimes to the police. Patrick also told the police that David wasn't involved in any of the murders, and didn't know about them.

Patrick was charged with twenty-one counts of murder, pleaded guilty, and was sentenced to twenty-one counts of life imprisonment. He is currently still serving his sentence in California.

CHAPTER 75: PEDRO ALONSO LOPEZ

The Monster of the Andes

Little eight-year-old Pedro was alone on the streets of a country in a civil war. He was hungry, tired, and cold. This was a nightmare for him. Things began to look up when an older man offered him food and shelter. The boy accepted immediately and became happy. Unfortunately, that is as far as the man's generosity went. He took the boy into an abandoned building, sodomized him many times, and then threw him back on the harsh street. It was the birth of "The Monster of the Andes."

Pedro Alonso Lopez was born on October 8, 1948. He was the seventh of thirteen children born to a prostitute. At the age of eight, his mother caught him fondling one of his younger sisters. This resulted in Pedro getting thrown out of the house, never to come back again. It was at this time that he was raped by that older man posing as a rescuer. This experience scarred Pedro for life, and he became very scared of strangers. He spent his time alone with barely enough food to stay alive. His luck became better when an American couple found him, offered him shelter and food, and put him in a day school for orphans. However, in 1963, when he was twelve, a male teacher sexually molested Pedro. Feeling trapped, he stole money from the school's office and ran away. His life of petty crimes started around this time. At age eighteen, he was stealing cars and selling his stolen items to chop shops. In 1969, he was caught and imprisoned for theft. In prison, he was gang raped by four older male prisoners.

Pedro's first murders occurred when he killed three of the four males who raped him. He received just two more years to his sentence for this, because the crimes were considered to be self-defense. His hatred towards women was fueled by his thoughts about his mother, and the pornographic magazines that he often looked at. He also blamed his mother for his misfortune in life.

Pedro was released in 1978. He travelled through Peru, Colombia, and Ecuador. He allegedly raped and killed 110 girls in Ecuador, more than 100 in Colombia, and 100 in Peru. He would lure innocent girls off the street to a secluded place. Sometimes he would take them to an already dug up grave. Then, he would brutally rape them and strangle them to death. He killed during the day so he would be able to see his victims' eyes as they faded away. Sometimes, he would spend the night talking to his "little friends," the corpses, and when they didn't talk back, he went searching for another victim. On average, he killed three girls each week.

One time, while trying to lure a girl from an Indian tribe, he was caught by the tribe members, who threatened to torture and kill him. However, an American missionary persuaded them to hand him over to the authorities. Pedro escaped death, and was never even imprisoned for the incident.

The authorities were aware of the high rate of missing girls, but they thought that they had been taken by an unknown gang to be sold as sex slaves. The case was never thoroughly investigated, and Pedro was able to go on killing undetected.

When a flash flood in Ecuador revealed the corpses of four children who were missing in April of 1980, the authorities were alerted. They knew then that they had a serial killer on their hands. Soon after, Pedro tried to lure a twelve-year-old girl away when her mother intervened. Pedro was chased and then the police arrested him.

Once he was caught, Pedro refused to cooperate. The police made a plan to dress a local priest as an inmate and put him in the cell with Pedro. Soon, Pedro started bragging about his killings, and horrifying facts were discovered. Pedro, under pressure from the police who acquired new information from the priest, eventually confessed to hundreds of murders. At first, the police didn't believe him, but then he directed them to a grave containing fifty-three bodies. Pedro was charged and sentenced to life imprisonment. However, in the summer of 1998, he was released. His whereabouts are currently unknown. During an exclusive interview before his release, Pedro stated that if he were ever released, he would kill again.

CHAPTER 76: PEDRO RODRIGUES FILHO

aka Pedrinho Matador

It is said that one of the happiest moments in a man's life is when his wife is pregnant and is about to give birth. An expecting father takes care of his wife and is afraid for anything to happen to her. She is bearing his child! This was not the case with Pedro's father, and the day Pedro was born, a killer was also born.

Pedro Rodrigues Filho was born in the year 1954. He was Brazilian, born in a farm in Santa Rita do Sapucaí. His father was very violent, and used to beat his wife even when she was pregnant with Pedro. This resulted in Pedro being born with a fractured skull. As early as thirteen years old, Pedro had urges to kill. Once he was fighting with his older cousin, and he pushed him to a sugar cane press. His cousin almost died, but luckily, he lived.

Pedro committed his first murder when he was just fourteen. His father was working as a school guard when he was accused of stealing food from the school's kitchen, thus he was fired. Pedro murdered the vice

Mayor of Alfenas, Minas Gerais. Later, Pedro murdered another guard, possibly the real thief who was stealing.

After that, Pedro ran away and hid in Mogi das Cruzes, São Paulo. There, he began stealing himself, and killed a drug dealer. He met Maria Aparecida Olympia, a woman he eventually lived with. Gang members killed her and Pedro sought her revenge. He killed many people in his search for revenge. At eighteen, he had already murdered ten people and injured several others.

His father eventually murdered Pedro's mother with a machete. While still in hiding in Mogi das Cruzes, he killed his father in revenge for the death of his mother. After killing him, he cut his heart out and ate a piece of it.

On May 24, 1973, Pedro was arrested. While serving his prison sentence, he killed around forty-seven inmates. He claimed that he had killed 100 victims; however, only seventy-one could be confirmed. In the year 2003, Pedro was sentenced to 126 years of imprisonment, and for his killings in prison, his sentence should have been extended to 400 years. However, the law in Brazil only allows for a maximum sentence of thirty years. He was scheduled for release in 2017, but he was released on April 24, 2007, after serving thirty-four years in prison.

After his release, he went to Fortaleza in Ceará. On September 15, 2011, he was again arrested. He was accused of false imprisonment and also starting a riot.

According to psychiatrics, Pedro suffered from post-traumatic stress disorder (PTSD). This may have resulted from him watching his father beating up his mother repeatedly. The reason behind his violence could be attributed to the injury he suffered before birth, and also the fact that he learned to be violent from his father.

CHAPTER 77: PETER BRYAN

Once upon a time, a man was cooking in his kitchen. Inside the pot on the stove was a human brain. This is not a scene from a Hannibal Lecter movie. Ten years ago, in February of 2004, in London, the neighbours of Peter Bryan heard a scream, and the police were called. When they caught Peter, they found that he had killed his friend, Brian Cherry, and he was in the process of cooking the victim's brain.

Peter Bryan was born in London on October 4, 1969. His parents were originally from Barbados, but they had immigrated to London before his birth. At the age of fifteen, he left school. He then got a job as a helper at the King's Road boutique.

He was caught stealing and fired from his job at the shop. On March 18, 1993, Peter got his revenge. He hit the daughter of the shop's owner, twenty-year-old Nisha Sheth, on the head with a hammer. She died before the arrival of ambulance. After admitting that he had killed Nisha, he was sent to the Rampton Secure Hospital and admitted to the psychiatric unit with maximum security. Peter was able to hide his insanity and appear normal. In fact, he was able to fool the doctors many times over the years.

Peter was released from the Rampton Hospital nine years later. In June 2001, he was transferred to the John Howard Center, under the care of a social worker and a psychiatrist. About a year later, he moved to the Riverside Hostel, where he was allowed to come and go whenever he pleased. The psychiatrist believed he could see an improvement in Peter's behaviour. In 2004, he was transferred to the Newham General Hospital's Topaz Ward. On February 17, he was given permission to leave the ward whenever he wanted. The same night, he went to forty-three-year-old Brian Cherry's house and killed him. He dismembered the body and laid out the pieces on the floor. Neighbours alerted the police after hearing screams coming from Brian's unit. When the police arrived, they found Peter covered in blood. He was frying the brain of his victim in a pan. He had killed Brian with twenty-four blows to his skull with a hammer.

Peter was arrested, and on April 15, 2004, he was sent to the maximum security Hospital of Broadmoor. Soon, doctors again thought that Peter was getting better, and he could be moved to a medium security ward. On April 25, 2004, Peter took the life of his third and final dupe, Richard Loudwell (age sixty). Richard was also a patient in the Broadmoor Hospital who was admitted for the murder of an eighty-two-year-old woman. In the dining room, Peter tried to strangle Richard, and then he smashed Richard's head on the floor. Due to the severe head injuries, Richard died on June 15. Peter also wanted to eat his victim, but neither had time nor the equipment to do so.

On March 15, 2005, Peter pleaded guilty for the murders of Brian and Richard. He was sentenced to life imprisonment without the chance of ever getting released again. He was found to be suffering from paranoid schizophrenia. He believes that cannibalism is normal. Perhaps the most terrifying aspect of the case is Peter's ability to appear to be a normal person, when in fact he is a very dangerous killer.

CHAPTER 78: PETER WILLIAM SUTCLIFFE

aka Yorkshire Ripper

Less than 100 years after the horror that struck London because of Jack the Ripper, another ripper emerged, this time in Yorkshire. The mutilated bodies of prostitutes were turning up, and for about five years, the killer would run freely.

Peter William Sutcliffe was born on June 2, 1946, in Yorkshire at West Riding. John William Sutcliffe was his father and Kathleen Frances Sutcliffe was his mother. He was the first of six children of a working class Catholic family.

At school, Peter was a loner. In secondary school, he was constantly bullied because he was too shy even to talk to girls, and not very interested in sports. He left school at the age of fifteen. He spent two years working in different jobs until he got an engineering apprenticeship. A few weeks later, he dropped out. He later started working as a gravedigger, but was fired due to his constant tardiness. In 1975, he worked as a long distance truck driver.

On Valentine's Day in 1967, Peter built up the courage to approach Sonia Szurma, and they got married in August 1974. They tried to have children many times, but couldn't. Believing that his wife was cheating on him, Peter began frequenting prostitutes. He started his violence in 1969, when he attacked a prostitute with a sock filled with stones. She was able to survive the attack, but she chose not to press any charges. Thirty-five-year-old Anna Rogulskyj was another lucky victim. Peter attacked her with a hammer and used a knife to slash her in 1975. When a witness heard the noise from the attack, Peter ran, and the victim survived.

Peter's first murder victim was twenty-eight-year-old Wilma McCann, whom he killed on October 30, 1975. Peter hit her two times on her skull with a hammer, and then he stabbed her in the abdomen, chest, and neck fifteen times. His second victim was Emily Jackson (age forty-two), murdered on January 20, 1976. Peter hit her with a hammer. Then, he stabbed her with a screwdriver fifty-two times in her lower abdomen, breasts, neck, and back. On February 5, 1977, Irene Richardson (age twenty-eight) was killed. Peter used a hammer to bludgeon her to death, and then mutilated her body with a sharp knife. A few months later, on April 23, he killed thirty-two-year-old Patricia Atkinson in her flat with a blow to her head using a hammer and after that, he stabbed her five times. On June 26, he murdered Jayne McDonald (age sixteen) by striking her in the head with a hammer and stabbing her in the chest and back twenty times. After trying to kill Maureen Long and getting interrupted,

He murdered Jean Jordan (age twenty) on October 1, by striking her eleven times with the help of a hammer, stabbing her eighteen times, and then after some days he dismembered her body because he couldn't find $5.00 that he had given her and believed that it was traceable.

Peter killed nine more women after that. On January 21, he beat Yvonne Pearson (age twenty-one) with a boulder. Ten days later, he raped Helen Rytka (age eighteen), beat her with a hammer, and stabbed her. On May 16, He beat Vera Milward (age forty) with a hammer, and after she died, he stabbed her. On April 4, 1979, Peter beat Josephine Whitaker (age nineteen), stabbed her twenty-seven times, and violated her sexually with a screwdriver. On September 2, Barbara Leach (age twenty) was beaten with a hammer and stabbed using a screwdriver. On August 20, 1980, Marguerite Walls (age thirty-seven) was also beaten with a hammer, after which he strangled her with a rope. On November 17, Peter beat Jacqueline Hill (age twenty) with a hammer and stabbed her in the eye and chest with a screwdriver.

The police were trying hard to find the killer but were misled by a series of phone calls from someone claiming that he was the ripper. Peter was actually interviewed nine times during the investigation. On January 2, 1981, the police stopped Peter again. His car had false number plates. He was questioned about the murders due to his physical resemblance to the killer, a description obtained through investigation. The police found incriminating evidence on the scene where he was arrested, and searched his house. On January 4, Peter confessed and gave details to his murders. The next day he was charged. He pleaded not guilty by reason of insanity, but was found guilty and sentenced to a minimum of thirty years in prison. On July 16, 2010, his sentence was changed to life imprisonment without parole.

CHAPTER 79:
RANDY STEVEN
KRAFT

On May 14, 1983, two police officers were patrolling the California Highway as usual. At 1:00 in the morning, they stopped a car under suspicion of drunk driving. The driver didn't wait in the car—instead, he stepped out. Although he denied being drunk, signs of intoxication were apparent, and he was arrested. One of the officers approached the car and saw a man apparently sleeping in the back. The officer knocked on the car's window but there was no response. He opened the door and discovered that the man was dead.

On March 19, 1945, Randolph Steven "Randy" Kraft was born in Long Beach. Randy had three older sisters. His family wasn't rich, and his mother had to take various jobs to complement his father's salary. His mother and three sisters loved Randy dearly. His father worked a lot and wasn't home much. In 1948, the family moved to Midway City in California.

In school, Randy was very intelligent, with a tested IQ of 129. As he grew up, he became interested in politics and wanted to become a future U.S. senator. At first, he was a conservative and a Republican. After high school, he attended the Claremont Men's College where he studied economics. During his third year, he abandoned his Republican views, and became a Democrat who was involved in the campaigns of Robert F. Kennedy. In his last year, he started drinking, doing drugs, and he had to repeat one course to earn his degree. He then enlisted in the U.S. Air Force, but after he came out as gay, he was discharged for "medical" reasons.

Randy is believed to have killed sixty-seven victims between the ages of thirteen and thirty-five. The murders occurred between 1971 and 1983. He was one of the three serial killers who, at the time, were believed to be a singular killer dubbed "the Freeway Killer." His victims were males, hitchhikers, runaways, or men he met in gay bars. He also chose men who were marines.

Randy would lure his victims to his car with a promise of a lift or alcohol. After the victim was in his car, he got them drunk and drugged them, usually with alcohol and Valium. Then, Randy tortured his victims by burning him with the car's cigarette lighter, emasculated them (before or after their death), sexually abused them, and sometimes inserted objects, like a sock, into their rectums. He would also bite his victims on or near the genitals or nipples. After all the torture, Randy strangled his victims to death, or killed them with drugs and more torture. He also took pictures of his victims in pornographic poses.

One of his most gruesome murders was that of twenty-two-year-old Mark Hall. He abducted his victim and drove him to a secluded canyon. Randy then tied Mark to a tree, sodomized, and emasculated him.

He then put the victim's genitals into his rectum. He also burned Mark on his chest, nose, scrotum, cheeks, and even destroyed his eyes with the lighter. With a broken bottle, he caused incisions to Mark's legs. Mark died of asphyxiation from earth and leaves that Randy had lodged into his trachea. It is believed that Mark was alive during the entire torture.

After his arrest for drunk driving on May 14, 1983, police searched Randy's car and apartment. Many prescription drugs were found, as well as clothes, and personal possessions incriminating Randy. In his car, a coded list was found that is believed to refer to each of his victims. The list contained sixty-one names, but the police couldn't identify them all. So much evidence was gathered against Randy. He was charged with sixteen murders, as well as counts of sodomy and torture. On September 26, 1988, Randy's trial began and it lasted for thirteen months. He was found guilty of all charges and sentenced to death. On August 11, 2000, his sentence was upheld by the California Supreme Court. He is still incarcerated at the San Quentin State Prison.

It is believed that Randy had an accomplice for some of his murders who went undetected. However, this has never been confirmed.

CHAPTER 80:
RICHARD ANGELO

Richard longed to become a hero so much that he inflicted near death experiences on his patients in order to save them. However, some of his patients walked the road until the end where they met death and couldn't be saved.

Richard Angelo was born on August 29, 1962. His father was a high school guidance counsellor. He worked for the Lindenhurst school district. His mother was a teacher of economics. Richard graduated high school in 1980, and enrolled in a two-year nursing program in which he was an honour student. He was an Eagle Scout, and after graduating high school was a volunteer fireman. It was revealed later that he had the Hero Syndrome. He would have done anything to be regarded as a hero. He even would go so far as killing.

Richard took a job at the Good Samaritan Hospital in Long Island, New York. His first known murder was of John Fisher in April 1987. He attempted to poison him in order to save him but failed, and John died. Between September 16 and October 11 of the same year, Richard was successful in poisoning six patients and killing them; two of these patients were poisoned on the same day.

Richard used the drugs Pavulon and Anectine. He would inject these paralyzing drugs into the patients' IV tubes, assuring them that he was giving them something to make them "feel better." When the patient went into cardiac arrest (he would wait until they were in a critical situation), Richard intervened and, as a hero, offered his expertise to save the patient. However, most of the time, the patients died. In the seven months during which he worked at the hospital, he murdered between ten and twenty-five patients, and poisoned more than twenty-five patients who luckily survived.

Richard's last victim was Gerolamo Kucich. On October 11, 1987, Richard injected the patient with the drugs. Gerolamo started feeling numb, but he had enough strength to push the call button and summon another nurse to help him. The nurse arrived after Richard had fled. The nurse took a urine sample of the man, and analyzed it. The tests showed traces of Anectine and Pavulon in the samples. Neither of these drugs had been subscribed to Gerolamo. The patient provided a description of the nurse who injected him, which matched Richard's appearance. The next day, the police searched Richard's locker and home. They found stashes of the drugs. Richard was then arrested and charged with first-degree assault of Gerolamo Kucich. The bodies of recently dead patients were exhumed and examined. Traces of the drugs were found in at least ten of the dead patients. Richard then confessed to the murders. His motive was that he wanted to emerge as a hero, saving the patients.

His lawyers tried to prove that Richard suffered from multiple personality disorder and that he did not have control over the actions of the other person-alities. However, the jury was not convinced. In De-cember of 1989, Richard was convicted of two counts of second-degree murder, second-degree manslaughter, six counts of assault, and one count of criminally neg-ligent homicide. He is suspected to have been respon-sible for many more killings. Richard was sentenced to sixty-one years to life in prison.

CHAPTER 81: RICHARD CHASE

"Someone stole my pulmonary artery," "my stomach is backwards," "my heart stopped beating"... these were the thoughts of Richard as he was seeking help at the hospital. When no one would offer help for these problems, he took the matters into his own hands.

Richard Trenton Chase was born on March 23, 1950. He had one sister who was four years younger than him. His father was strict, and his parents would often quarrel. By the age of ten, Richard was also a bed-wetter, enjoyed torturing and killing animals, and he also liked setting things on fire, thus completing the Macdonald triad.

During his adolescence, he became an alcoholic and often used drugs. He also had erectile dysfunction, which affected his relationships with girls. At eighteen, he sought psychiatric help to his problem, which was rooted to a mental illness. As an adult, he became a hypochondriac, even believing that his mother was trying to poison him. He moved in with some roommates who thought that he was weird. Annoyed by his abuse of drugs and alcohol and his inappropriate behaviour, his roommates asked him to move out. When he refused, they left themselves. He was forced to move back in with his parents, but then they found him an apartment and paid his rent. At that time, Richard was still killing animals, but now he was also consuming their raw organs and drinking their blood. He believed that he needed it because his blood was turning into powder. In 1975, he was admitted into the hospital due to blood poisoning. He was treated with psychotropic drugs and released a year later into his parents' care. His mother stopped giving him his antipsychotic medicine because she believed that it made him lazy, and moved him into an apartment alone. There, Richard realized that animal blood was not enough and he had to start consuming human blood.

His first murder was of Ambrose Griffin (age fifty-one) whom he shot in a drive-by shooting. Ambrose was his driveway helping his wife with the groceries. Later, Richard would commit a series of break-ins. On January 11, 1978, Richard asked his neighbour for a cigarette. She gave him one, but he wouldn't let her walk away until she gave him the entire pack. Two weeks later, he broke into the house of Robert and Barbara Edwards. They walked into their house and heard a noise, which turned out to be Richard. He was able to run away, however. He had urinated in a drawer that contained baby clothing, and defecated on a child's bed. Richard later stated that he often tried to open doors in his neighbourhood. He believed that locked doors were a sign that he was not wanted, but an unlocked door was an invitation for him to enter.

On January 23, 1978, Richard committed a gruesome murder. Twenty-two-year-old Teresa Wallin was in her third month of pregnancy. She was taking out the garbage when Richard encountered her. He shot her three times with the same gun used in his first murder, then dragged the body to her bedroom. There, he raped her body, and stabbed her many times with a butcher knife. He removed some of her organs, cut off one nipple, and drank her blood. Before he left, he put dog feces in her mouth and pushed it down her throat. Her husband discovered her body later.

A few days later, Richard committed his final murders. Evelyn Miroth (age thirty-eight) was babysitting her nephew, David Ferreira (age twenty-two months). Her six-year-old son, Jason, and her friend, Daniel Meredith (age fifty-one), were also in her house at the time. Richard shot Daniel in the head in the hallway. In Evelyn's bedroom, he shot Jason in the head two times. Evelyn was raped postmortem and sodomized many times. Richard cut out her stomach and removed several organs. He cut her throat, and stabbed her repeatedly in the anus. He also tried to remove one eyeball.

The body of David was not found on the scene. Apparently, Richard had been interrupted by a knock on the door. He took the baby with him, decapitated him, and ate some of his organs. The body was later found mutilated in a box at a nearby church.

Richard was not an organized serial killer, and he left many pieces of evidence (like hand and shoe prints) that led to his arrest. Richard first denied the killings, but in the end confessed. He was charged with six counts of murder, and pleaded guilty by reason of insanity.

He was found guilty of all counts and sentenced to death in the gas chamber. While in prison, inmates tried to talk him into killing himself. On December

26, 1980, Richard was found dead from an overdose of medication.

CHAPTER 82: RICHARD RAMIREZ

Aka Night Stalker

In 1985, "The Night Stalker" terrorized the streets of Los Angeles. With fourteen murder victims, Richard Ramirez was one of the most prolific serial killers that the U.S. has ever witnessed.

Ricardo Leyva "Richard" Muñoz Ramírez was born on February 29, 1960, in El Paso, Texas. His parents, Julian and Mercedes, had four other children before him: Ruben, Joseph, Robert, and Ruth. Due to the chemical fumes that his mother inhaled while pregnant with him at her job, the pregnancy was difficult. When he was two, Richard suffered from a concussion when a dresser fell on him.

Richard was a loner. In fifth grade, it was discovered that he suffered from epilepsy, which resulted in getting him removed from being a quarterback on the school's football team. When he was only ten, he started smoking marijuana and spending nights at the local cemetery. At twelve, his cousin Miguel came back from Vietnam after completing his second tour. Miguel showed Richard pictures of women he had tortured and raped before killing them. Richard was taught how to kill with stealth. When Richard was thirteen, Miguel shot and killed his wife right in front of him. Richard started his criminal life of petty theft, burglarizing, and cannabis addiction. His brother Ruben also taught Richard more about stealing. During his teen years, he became interested in Satan, and would later become a worshipper. At eighteen, he moved to Los Angeles.

During his lifetime, he committed fourteen murders and several thefts, rapes, and attempted murders. On June 28, 1984, Richard broke into the home of Jennie Vincow (age seventy-nine). After not finding anything valuable to steal, he became enraged and stabbed Jennie and slit her throat. Then, he performed necrophilia with the corpse. On March 17, 1985, Richard shot Angela Barrio (age twenty-two) outside her condo. On the same day, he pulled Tsai-Lian Yu (age thirty) out of her car, and shot her several times. She died before the ambulance could arrive. Three days later, he killed an eight-year-old girl.

On March 27, Richard shot Vincetn Zazarra (age sixty-four) and his wife Maxine (age forty-four). He then mutilated the wife's body after her death. Two months later, Richard shot Harold Wu (age sixty-six) in his head. Then, he punched his wife Jean Wu (age sixty-three) and raped her brutally, but let her live. There was now a description to the killer: he was Hispanic, had long, dark hair, and had a foul smell.

On May 29, 1985, he killed Malvial Keller (age eighty-three) with a hammer, and assaulted her sister Blanche Wolfe (age eighty) who was invalid, and survived. On the scene, he used lipstick to draw a pentagram on Malvial's thigh and on the wall of the bedroom.

On May 30, Richard raped Ruth Wilson (age forty-one) and sodomized her. Her son who was only twelve years old was locked in the closet. Richard then slashed Ruth.

His series of rapes and murders continued. Between June 27 and August 8, 1985, Richard killed seven more victims. On August 24, he shot Bill Carns (age twenty-nine), and raped his fiancée, Inez Erickson (age twenty-seven), but left her alive. She was able to give a description of him and the car that he was driving to police.

The police were able to locate Richard's abandoned car, and get a fingerprint from the rear-view mirror. They got a match, and "The Night Stalker" was identified. On August 30, 1985, an arrest warrant was issued, and his picture was released to the public.

Richard walked into a liquor store where a woman recognized him and shouted, "The Night Stalker!" He ran away, but a mob was formed and pursued him. He tried to steal a man's car, but the mob closed in on him, captured him, and waited for the police to come and arrest him.

On September 20, 1989, after a four-year trial with many complications, Richard was convicted of thirteen murders, five attempted murders, eleven sexual assaults, and fourteen burglaries. He was given the death penalty. He had many female fans during his stay in prison. On June 7, 2013, Richard died of liver failure.

CHAPTER 83: ROBERT BERDELLA

It was Saturday morning of Easter weekend in 1988 when the police in Kansas City, Missouri, received a strange call. A naked man was running around the neighbourhood. The patrol unit in that area went to investigate. The man, twenty-two-year-old Chris Bryson, was wearing nothing but a dog collar. His story was shocking.

Robert Andrew "Bob" Berdella was born on January 31, 1949, in Cuyahoga Falls, Ohio. He was raised as a Catholic but he stopped attending church in his teen years. His father often beat him with a leather strap. His brother Daniel, who was younger than he by seven years, was his father's favourite. Bob had a hard time in school, but he worked hard and did very well. Unfortunately, he was bullied. At the age of five, he started wearing thick glasses because he was nearsighted. At sixteen, his father died from a heart attack at the age of thirty-nine. His mother went on to remarry. Around this time, he would later claim that a coworker sexually assaulted him at the restaurant he worked. The movie adaptation of John Fowles' *The Collector* had a great effect on him. In 1967, he got into the Kansas City Art Institution, and would later start a career as a successful chef.

During that time, he also began torturing animals and experimenting on them. In addition, he was abusing alcohol and selling drugs. At nineteen, he was arrested for possession but released. At thirty-two, he quit his work as a chef and opened his own antique store called Bob's Bizarre Bazaar. He was an openly gay man who, after a failed relationship, had started spending time with male prostitutes. He also tried to help them out.

The killings started in July of 1984. Robert drugged a male prostitute named Jerry Howell (age twenty); he was Robert's friend. He kept him in the basement where he tortured him and raped him over and over again. He died from asphyxiation the next day. On April 10, 1985, Robert Sheldon (age eighteen), who was also Robert's friend, wanted to stay with him. However, Bob also drugged him and kept him in the basement where he also tortured him. On April 15, Bob had to kill him by suffocation when a man came to work on the house.

On June 22, 1985, Bob offered shelter to Mark Wallace (age twenty). Mark was also drugged and kept captive. Bob tortured him for hours before killing him. On September 26, Bob picked up James Ferris (age twenty-five) from a gay bar. James was tortured for weeks and then was killed. On June 17, 1986, another victim was claimed. Bob lured Todd Stoops (age twenty-one) to his house. He tortured him in the basement for six weeks before killing him. Another victim of the same type of torture was Larry Pearson (age twenty), claimed on July 9, 1987.

Bob tortured his victims by puncturing their

anal cavities with his fist, using electrical shocks on them, applying bleach to their eyes with cotton swabs, and sometimes injecting their vocal cords with drain cleaner. Once, Bob tried to gouge the eyes out of a victim. After his victims were dead, he cleaned them, dismembered their bodies, and disposed of them by leaving them for trash pick up. Bob also documented his torture with Polaroid pictures and notes. He would sometimes give the victim antibiotics to last longer. He also sometimes kept the head of his victims as a trophy, and he buried one in the backyard.

Bob's last victim was Chris Bryson, whom he captured on March 29, 1988. However, after days of torture, Chris was able to escape by jumping from the second floor window naked. He told the story of his torture to the police. Bob was arrested, but first the police thought it was a lover's quarrel. After the investigation, and the search of his house, they found evidence of the tortures and murders. To avoid the death penalty, Bob provided the police with a full confession. He was sentenced to life imprisonment. While serving his sentence, Bob died of a heart attack in 1992.

CHAPTER 84: ROBERT CHARLES BROWN

"Seven sacred virgins, entombed side by side, those less worthy, are scattered wide," the letter says. *"The score is you 1, the other team 48. If you were to drive to the end zone in a white Trans Am, the score could be 9 to 48. That would complete your home court sphere."* This was a letter sent by Robert Brown to the El Paso County prosecutors in 2000. The story had begun some decades ago.

Robert Charles Brown was born on October 31, 1952, in Coushatta, Louisiana. He had eight siblings. On New Year's Eve of 1961, his grandfather threw himself in a well. Two years later, his aunt was brutally murdered. At the age of sixteen, Robert dropped out of high school. He then joined the United States Army, and served from 1969 to 1976. Due to his drug abuse, he was dishonourably discharged from the army. During his lifetime, Robert was married many times: Terry Laverne Ward, from 1970 to 1973; Tuyet Minh Huynh, from 1973 to 1976 (he had a son named Thomas with her in 1974); Brenda Gayle Ware, from 1977 to 1980 (he beat her brutally and she barely survived); Rita Coleman, from 1980 to 1984 (he strangled her and almost crushed her larynx; during that time he was also arrested many times for stealing); and Diane Marcia Babbitts, in 1988. During his years, Robert abused alcohol and drugs. He also tortured animals and set them on fire.

Robert claimed to have killed at least forty-eight victims in a period that ranges from 1970 to 1995. His first confirmed victim was Heather Dawn Church (age thirteen). Heather lived with her parents Mike and Diane in a remote property outside Colorado Springs. She had three brothers, and was an excellent child. Her parents later separated, and her father moved out. Thirty-eight-year-old Robert was their neighbour up the road at the time. On September 17, 1991, Diane took two of her sons to a Boy Scout meeting. Heather was left to babysit her five-year-old brother. After the meeting, Diane returned home and could not find Heather anywhere. She called everyone she knew, and even Heather's father, but no one knew anything about her daughter. The police were called, and a search started the next day. Diane remembered that there was an open window in the master bedroom. The police examined the window, which appeared to have been forced open, and they were able to lift a fingerprint. They ran the fingerprint but couldn't find any match in the database of convicted offenders. At that time, the databases across states weren't yet linked. The investigation continued, and they questioned everyone, including Robert. It wasn't until two years later that Heather's remains were found.

Four years after Heather's murder, Detective Lou Smit reopened the case. He kept looking at the case from every angle. He ran the fingerprint again, and this time got a hit from Louisiana. The man was Robert Charles Brown, Heather's neighbour at that time. Robert was then brought in for questioning. At first, he claimed his innocence. As other cases were being investigated again, he pleaded guilty for the murder of Heather to avoid the death penalty, and received a life sentence.

After his letter, which was sent in 2000, the detectives pursued more clues given by Robert. In the end, they were able to link him to the disappearance and murder of fifteen-year-old Rocio Delpilar Sperry, who had been killed in 1987. Again, Robert received another life sentence.

Robert claims that he murdered forty-eight victims. However, his claims could not be verified, and it is believed he may have claimed this high number of victims just to set a record.

CHAPTER 85:
ROBERT PICKTON

If no bodies were discovered, then the murders never happened. These were probably the thoughts of Robert Pickton when he found a clever way to dispose of his victims' bodies: he fed them to the pigs. He was in possession of a death farm!

Robert William "Willie" Pickton was born on October 24, 1949, in Vancouver, British Columbia. Not much is known about his childhood, teen years, or young adult years. In the 1970s, his parents died and left him (along with his brother, David Francis Pickton, and sister, Linda Louise Wright) the pig farm that had been in the family for three generations. Between 1994 and 1995, they sold parts of the land to shopping centres and housing estates, making millions from the sales. He had a social club named "Piggy's Palace" to which he would procure prostitutes by luring them with a promise of drinks, money, or drugs. However, Robert did not drink or smoke. His neighbours later remembered him as a hardworking man.

In 1997, Robert tried to stab a prostitute named Wendy Lynn Eistetter. He was charged with attempted murder, and although there was evidence incriminating him, the charges were dropped because the prosecutors thought that the victim couldn't give an accurate testimony because she was a drug addict.

A large number of women who were prostitutes, Aboriginals, or drug addicts disappeared from the streets of Vancouver in the 1980s. However, the missing women went largely unnoticed and since no bodies had been found, there was no public pressure to start an investigation. The official investigation didn't start until 1998.

Robert is believed to have killed forty-nine women. Since it is still an ongoing investigation, the ways of his killings are still not fully known. However, it is widely believed that he lured his victims with promises of drugs and money. Then, after sex, he strangled or shot his victims. Later, he would put the remains in a wood chipper, and feed them to the pigs on the farm.

On February 5, 2002, the police obtained a warrant for a firearm violation. Robert was arrested. On the farm, the police found several personal items belonging to one of the missing women. They obtained another court order, and were able to search the farm thoroughly. During the search, the police found some remains of the victims like half cut skulls, human feet and hands stuffed in the skulls, the DNA of thirty-three women, clothing with blood on it that belonged to one victim, and a jawbone and teeth that all belonged to another victim. One .22 revolver with a dildo attached to its barrel (acting like a silencer), rounds from a .357 Magnum, handcuffs, night vision goggles, and photos of a trash can with human remains of one victim were also found.

An undercover cop posing as an inmate was

placed in the same cell as Robert after his arrest. Robert told him he had killed forty-nine women, and that he needed only one more to make it an even fifty. His trial started on January 30, 2006, and a video recording of Robert's confession to his "fellow inmate" was used as evidence.

Robert was charged with twenty-seven (then twenty-six, for lack of evidence) first-degree murders, but he pleaded not guilty. Publication was banned, so not all the details are known. However, for the first six processed murders of Georgina Faith Papin, Sereena Abostway, Andrea Joesbury, Mona Lee Wilson, Marnie Lee Frey, and Brenda Ann Wolfe, he was found guilty of second-degree murder, and was sentenced to life in prison on December 6, 2007, with a chance for parole in twenty-five years as the Canadian law entails. There were twenty additional charges added on August 4, 2010. Two appeals were made by the defense, but both were rejected. One appeal by the prosecution was allowed, on the grounds of mistakenly excluding some evidence and splitting the charges. Currently, Robert Pickton remains in prison.

CHAPTER 86: ROSEMARY WEST

As a wife of a murderer, Rose also became a life taker. With her husband Fred, together they raped and killed many women, including their daughters.

Rosemary Pauline "Rose" West (née Letts) was born on November 29, 1953, in Devon, England. Her father was violent, and her mother suffered from depression. While she was pregnant, her mother had electroconvulsive therapy for her depression. This may have caused some injuries in Rose, which made her "slow." Rose didn't perform well in school, and was made fun of by other children. Growing up, she had weight problems, was aggressive, and was sexually promiscuous. She developed a sexual interest in older men.

Her father would often beat everyone in the family, and her mother would often take the beatings. There also rumours that her father sexually assaulted her and that they became involved in incest. This is why, her mother moved out of the home, and took Rose with her. However, Rose soon returned to live with her father. On November 29, 1968, Rose met Fred West. A year later, they moved in together, although her father did not approve. On October 17, 1970, Rose gave birth to their daughter, Heather Ann. Shortly after, Fred was imprisoned for theft. Rose was left alone to take care of Heather, and Fred's two daughters from a previous marriage, Charmaine and Ann Marie.

Rose often beat the two girls in fits of rage. Just before the release of Fred, Rose killed Charmaine. After his release, they buried the body together. Fred cut off her toes, fingers, and kneecaps. When his ex-wife, Charmaine's mother, came to look for her, the couple also killed her. On January 29, 1972, Rose and Fred got married, and had their second daughter, Mae, on June 1. Later, Rose became a prostitute, inviting men to the house. She had seven more children, of which maybe only three were Fred's.

Together, the couple would bring home women (by luring them or hiring them as nannies). Rose helped Fred rape them, torture them, and kill them. Fred even sexually abused his own daughters. They also killed their daughter Heather when she told her friends about the abuse she was facing at home. In June 1987, sixteen-year-old Heather was strangled to death, dismembered, and buried in the garden. Their son, Stephen, was forced to help dig his sister's grave. Together, Fred and Rose killed ten victims.

Fred continued raping one of their daughters, and even videotaped himself doing it. She told her friend who told her mother. The police were called in. The police started investigating the rapes and soon charged the couple. However, the case collapsed when the daughter refused to testify. The police refused to give up and began looking into Heather's disappearance. They obtained a search warrant and excavated the garden behind the house. During the search, they discovered human bones. Fred was arrested on February 25, 1994. He later confessed to the murders, and while awaiting trial, hanged himself.

Rosemary did not confess, but there was a load of circumstantial evidence against her. In October 1995, she went on trial. On November 22, 1995, she was found guilty of ten murders. The judge sentenced her to life imprisonment, but the Lord Chief Justice decided that she would spend just twenty-five years in prison. In July 1997, she was subjected to whole life tariff. Rose maintains her innocence to this day.

CHAPTER 87: ROY NORRIS

"Make noise there, girl! Go ahead and scream or I'll make you scream!" This was heard on the tape Roy and Lawrence made recording one of their crimes. The girl died, but she wasn't the only one.

On February 2, 1948, Roy Lewis Norris was born. He was born in Greely, Colorado, and his mother was addicted to drugs and didn't want him. She put him in a caring centre where he would be moved around to live with many families. These families often neglected the children, and in one specific Hispanic family, he was sexually abused. At seventeen, Roy dropped out of high school and joined the Navy where he worked in San Diego. At twenty-one, he was sent to Vietnam but didn't see combat. There, he used marijuana and tried heroin, but only continued using marijuana. He went back to the states the same year.

Roy's first arrest was made on November 1969, for attempted rape. In February of 1970, while on bail, he attempted to break-in into a woman's house to rape her, but he was arrested again. Three months later, he was discharged from his duties after being diagnosed with a schizophrenic personality disorder. In May of 1970, also on bail, Roy bashed in the head of a female college student in San Diego, and then slammed her head into the street. He was arrested, found guilty for assault with a dangerous weapon, and sentenced with imprisonment of five years at the Atascadero State Hospital. He was also declared a mentally disabled sex offender. Three months after his release in 1975, he raped a woman. He was identified a month later. He was arrested and convicted again, and imprisoned in the Men's Colony of California in San Luis Obispo, where he met Lawrence Bittaker. Together, the two planned to rape and kill one teenage girl every month after their release.

After their release, Roy and Lawrence reunited. They soon figured out a way to apply their plan. At first, they bought a van, which they nicknamed "Murder Mack," and in June of 1979, they started practicing how to lure girls by picking up female hitchhikers, and they chose a secluded area to commit their crimes.

On June 24, 1979, they dragged Lucinda Lynn Schaeffer (age sixteen) into the van. They were able to bind her, take her to the location, and rape her one after the other. Her only request was to pray before she died, but Lawrence strangled her at once when they were done with her. She was wrapped with a plastic shower curtain and was tossed over a canyon for the animals.

On July 8, 1979, Andrea Hall (age eighteen) was hitchhiking to her boyfriend's when the pair picked her up. Roy took her to the back, subdued her, and also bound her ankles and ankles. She was raped in their chosen area. Lawrence humiliated her more by taking pictures, and forcing her to perform oral sex and beg for her life. He then stabbed an ice pick into her ears, piercing her brain. She was strangled while still conscious, and the corpse was dumped over a cliff.

On September 3, the pair took Jackie Gilliam (age fifteen) and Jacqueline Leah Lamp (age thirteen). They raped them over the course of two days, and Lawrence took pictures and tape-recorded himself during the rapes. Jackie was murdered by being stabbed in her ears with an ice pick and then strangled. Jacqueline was bludgeoned and strangled.

Their last victim was Shirley Lynette Ledford (age sixteen). They abducted her on October 31, 1979. For two hours, while driving in the van, the pair tortured, raped, and sodomized her, while recording their acts. Roy strangled her with a coat hanger, and they dumped her on a random lawn. She was discovered the next day.

Roy liked to brag about his crimes, so he told an old inmate friend named Jimmy Dalton who, in his turn, told his attorney, and then the authorities. He was able to give details about the crimes. One woman, Robin Robeck, who had been raped by the pair but survived, was able to identify them as the offenders. The two were put under surveillance. On November 20, 1979, they were arrested. Their apartment was searched, and the police found many items of incriminating evidence. Ten days after the arrest, Roy confessed. They were charged with five murders in February 1980. Roy accepted a plea bargain agreeing to testify against Lawrence and pled guilty in order to avoid the death penalty. On May 7, 1980, Roy was sentenced to forty-five years to life in prison. He applied for parole in 2010, but was denied.

CHAPTER 88:
RUSSELL WILLIAMS

Colonel David Russell Williams was once the pride of the country. However, something changed with the Colonel. He transformed from being a good leader into a sexual predator.

David Russell Williams was born on March 7, 1963, in Bromsgrove, England. His father was Cedric David Williams, a metallurgist, and his mother Christine Nonie Williams. His family immigrated to Canada and moved to Ontario, where his father worked in the first nuclear research laboratory. In 1970, his parents divorced. His mother married Jerry Sovka, and Russell took the name Sovka. He graduated high school in 1982.

Russell started his military career in 1987 when he enrolled in the Canadian Forces. In 1990, he was transferred to 3 Canadian Forces Flying Training School (3CFFTS). On January 1, 1991, he was promoted to Captain. By 1994, he was transporting VIPs in his post. He got married on June 1, 1991 to Mary Elizabeth Harriman, an associate director of the Heart and Stroke Foundation. In November of 1999, he was promoted again, to Major. After obtaining a master's degree in Defense Studies in 2004, he was promoted to Lieutenant

Colonel. In July 2006, Russell and his wife moved to Orleans. Russell served in many different posts during his career and was described as a "shining bright star." He was an elite pilot.

Russell's crime spree began in 2007. During this time, he started breaking into his neighbours' homes. He would enter the girls' rooms and try on their underwear. He also took pictures while posing in the underwear and, before leaving, he would steal some of the clothes. No one suspected that Colonel Williams would do such things. For the next couple of years, he kept this habit of breaking and entering, and stealing underwear after taking pictures wearing them. Soon, his crimes escalated. In 2009, he broke into two Soon, Soon, his crimes escalated. In 2009, he broke into two neighbourhood houses, attacked the women, and sexually assaulted them. He also took pictures.

The Colonel was still flying once a month. On many of his flights, Cpl. Marie-France Comeau (age thirty-eight) worked as a flight attendant. Russell broke into her home, beat her, and tied her to a pole. He then raped her repeatedly and recorded himself doing it. Marie-France begged for her life, but Russell covered her nose and her mouth with duct tape almost suffocating her, and took her to the bed upstairs to rape her again. She tried to escape but failed.

After he finished, he killed her calmly. He left a single shoe print in her blood. On November 25, 2009, her boyfriend found her dead body while the Colonel was at a fundraiser. Marie-France was buried on December 4. The Colonel sent a letter of condolence to the victim's father.

On January 28, 2010, Russell broke into the

house of Jessica Lloyd (age twenty-seven) while she was sleeping. She lived alone. He bound her, putting duct tape over her eyes. Then, he assaulted her, while taking pictures and video recording the assault. He raped her at her house, took her to his cottage, and raped her there again. He made her shower, and watched as she was shivering in the bathtub. He took pictures of her in lingerie. She begged for her life. She begged that he let her tell her mother that she loved her. Instead, Russell hit her with a flashlight from behind, and murdered her by strangulation. He dumped her body on a rural road near his cottage. The police were able to find her purse in the driveway, but her body wasn't located until February 8, 2010.

The police blocked the roads in search of Jessica. On February 4, the Colonel was stopped, and an officer noticed that the tires of his SUV matched the ones left by the SUV seen by a passerby parked next to Jessica's home on the night of her disappearance. On February 7, Russell was called in for questioning. After being told about the evidence linking him to Jessica's disappearance, Russell confessed. A search of his cottage led to finding the photos and videos linking him to all the crimes.

On October 18, 2010, his trial began. Russell pleaded guilty to two sexual assaults, two murders, and eighty-two break-ins. Three days later he was sentenced to two counts of life imprisonment, and 120 years for his other crimes.

CHAPTER 89: STEPHEN GRIFFITHS

"This is someone who was almost a wannabe serial killer. He wanted his 15 minutes in the spotlight." (David Wilson, a professor in Criminology, on Stephen Griffiths).

Stephen Shaun Griffiths was born on December 24, 1969, in West Yorkshire. His mother was Moira Dewhirst, a receptionist, and his father Stephen Griffiths, a frozen food salesman. He had two younger siblings. His father soon left them, but his mother managed to pay for Stephen's schooling. In his teenage years, Stephen began shoplifting. One time, when a manager tried to stop him from stealing, he attacked the man with a knife. At seventeen, he was sentenced to three years of youth custody. Stephen admitted to his probation officer that he fantasized about killing. In 1987, he was diagnosed as a schizoid psychopath.

In 1992, he received two years in prison for attacking a woman with a knife and holding it to her throat. Stephen earned a degree in psychology in his studies in Leeds University, and then at Bradford University, he started on his Ph.D. in criminology. Later, he became so interested in serial killers that he began buying books about them online. Then he bought a crossbow. At the age of twenty-seven, Stephen moved into a flat in Bradford, near a Thornton Road, an area frequented by prostitutes. He created an online pseudonym, "Ven Pariah," and posted using this nickname the night before one of his murders.

His first victim was Susie Rushworth (age forty-three), who was a mother and a grandmother. She was a prostitute and a drug addict who was trying to get clean. On June 22, 2009, Susie disappeared. Her body was never found. It is believed that Stephen beat her with a hammer until death. The only thing linking him to the murder was a trace of blood in his bathroom.

Stephen's second victim was thirty-one-year-old Shelley Armitage, who disappeared on April 26, 2010. She was also a prostitute and a drug addict with enemies. Only parts of her body were found, like parts of the shoulders, some connective tissue, and the vertebrae. When her cell phone turned up later, a video was found on it. It showed her naked body in a bathtub. She was then tied up and put on the bed. The words "My Sex Slave" were written on her back.

Stephen's last victim was Suzanne Blamires (age thirty-six). Suzanne disappeared on May 22, 2010. Although coming from a loving home, she became a prostitute (and was for ten years) after getting addicted to drugs and wanting to find a way to pay for it. Eighty-one fragments of Suzanne's body were found in the River Aire a few days after Stephen's arrest. Her skinless head was without nose or ears. Embedded in her skull was a crossbow arrow and knife fragments.

Stephen's last murder was caught on security camera in his own apartment complex. The footage showed a woman escaping an apartment, a man going after her, wrestling her to the ground, and shooting her with a crossbow twice to the head. Then, he dragged her back to the apartment. The man later left the apartment with large bags. Stephen was found easily. The police went into his apartment and searched it. They found enough evidence to incriminate him even without the footage on the security camera. They found video recordings, journals that he kept on the murders, crossbows with bloodstains on them, and about thirty knives.

Stephen claimed that he murdered more women, but only these three murders were confirmed. It is unlikely that he killed more because he could give details about these murders enthusiastically but wouldn't answer any questions about other murders. He bragged that he ate pieces of his victims, both cooked (in the case of the first two) and raw (in the case of the last victim).

In December 2010, Stephen pleaded guilty for his crimes. He was sentenced to life in prison. He did not show any regret or even emotion. However, while in prison, he attempted to commit suicide four times, and in 2011, he went on a hunger strike. He was later moved to Rampton Psychiatric Hospital in Nottinghamshire.

CHAPTER 90: THEODORE ROBERT BUNDY

aka Ted Bundy

Ted was a handsome and attractive guy. To his friends and family, he was normal and a good man. However, no one knew the dark side of Ted, the side who raped and murdered women.

Theodore Robert Cowell was born on November 24, 1946. His mother, Eleanor Louise Cowell, was not married. She moved in with her parents, and Ted was raised to believe that Louise was his older sister. In May 1951, Louise got married to Johnnie Culpepper Bundy, and Ted assumed the Bundy last name. He had four step-siblings.

Growing up, Ted was shy, but he excelled in school. Even in college, he kept to himself and rarely dated, until he met the woman of his dreams, Stephanie Brooks, and fell in love. However, in 1968, after graduating, Stephanie broke Ted's heart when she left him. He became depressed and dropped out of college, but continued to obsess about her. Around that time, he found out that Louise was actually his mother. His friends also began to suspect that Ted was a petty thief.

During this time in his life, his personality began to change. He became more confident, went back to college, and earned a degree in psychology. He was also interested in politics. At that time, he met Meg Anders (who later used the pseudonym Elizabeth Kendall for her book about Ted), a divorcee with a daughter, with whom he would date for five years. He was still obsessed with Stephanie, and would rekindle their relationship while still with Meg. However, in February 1974, Ted cut off all communication with Stephanie.

It is speculated that Ted's victim count is as high as 100 or more. His murders occurred between January 1974 and February 1978, in several different states.

In Washington, Ted killed eleven women: Lynda Ann Healy, aged twenty-one, murdered on February 1, 1974, bludgeoned; Donna Gail Manson, aged nineteen, murdered on March 12, 1974, abducted but body not found; Susan Elaine Rancourt, aged eighteen, murdered on April 17, 1974, abducted; Roberta Kathleen Parks, aged twenty-two, murdered on May 6, 1974, disappeared from Oregon State University; Brenda Carol Ball, aged twenty-two, disappeared on June 1, 1974; Georgeann Hawkins, aged eighteen, abducted on June 11, 1974; Janice Ann Ott, aged twenty-three, abducted on July 14, 1974; and Denise Marie Naslund, aged nineteen, abducted on July 14, 1974. Three other victims in Washington remain unidentified.

Eight of his victims were in Utah: Nancy Wilcox, aged sixteen, strangled on October 2, 1974; Melissa Anne Smith, aged seventeen, disappeared on October 18, 1974; Laura Ann Aime, aged seventeen, disappeared on October 31, 1974; Debra Kent, aged seventeen, vanished on November 8, 1974, after leaving a school play; and Susan Curtis, aged fifteen, disappeared on June 28, 1975. Three additional victims remain unidentified.

In Colorado, three were murdered: Caryn Campbell, aged twenty-three, disappeared on January 12, 1975, body found on a dirt road; Julie Cunningham, aged twenty-six, disappeared on March 15, 1975, body not found; and Denise Oliverson, aged twenty-five, abducted on April 6, 1975.

There were two victims in Idaho, but only one identified as twelve-year-old Lynette Culver, who was abducted on May 6, 1975.

There were three victims in Florida as well. Ted attacked a sorority house on January 15, 1978, assaulting five girls and killing two of them: Margaret Bowman, aged twenty-one, and Lisa Levy, aged twenty. Both women were strangled as they slept. Twelve-year-old Kimberly Diane Leach was another Florida victim; Ted abducted her on February 9, 1978.

Ted also killed two unidentified victims in Oregon, and one unidentified victim in California. Sometimes, he lured the women to his car by pretending that he needed help, often wearing a cast as if his arm was broken. He used his attractiveness and charm to lure the women.

In August 1975, Ted was arrested after trying to get away from a driving violation. He was at first only suspected of attempted burglary, but evidence linked to the murders. In February 1976, he was sentenced to fifteen years for attempted kidnapping, and later charged with murder. In June 1977, during his pretrial, he managed to escape. However, he was recaptured a week later. On December 30, he was able to escape again, and fled to Florida where he committed more murders.

A week after his last kill, Ted was arrested again for driving a stolen vehicle. Physical evidence was found linking him to the murders, as well as witnesses. He went on two different trials for the murders he committed in Florida. He received three death sentences. On January 24, 1989, Ted Bundy died in the electric chair, and the crowds cheered.

CHAPTER 91: THOMAS QUICK

A serial killer or a compulsive liar? The truth about Thomas is lost. Although convicted of many murders, some critics believe that he actually never killed anyone.

Sture Ragnar Bergwall was born on April 26, 1950, in Korsnäs, Falun, Sweden. He was also known as Thomas Quick (Thomas the name of his first victim, and Quick is his mother's maiden name).

Thomas claimed that he had a rough childhood, with his father sexually abusing him and his mother physically abusing him. However, his brother claims that these were all lies. He also claimed that at the age of fourteen, he and a man in his twenties drove around looking for boys for Thomas to sodomize and the man liked to watch.

In the early 1990s, Thomas was in a closed psychiatric confinement when he began confessing to murders. According to him, his first murder was of Thomas Blomgren in Växjö, in 1964. Thomas was only fourteen, and allegedly, his victim was the same age. Thomas took his victim to the woods where he strangled him to death. He also confessed to the murder of Alvar Larsson, whom he drowned in the lake Åsnen in Urshult. However, Thomas's sister reports that her brother never left Falun at that time. Thomas confessed to more than thirty murders in all, but was convicted of only eight of them:

- Charles Zelmanovits in 1976;
- Johan Asplund in 1980;
- The Stegehuis couple in 1984 (Thomas was able to give information about this case that wasn't made public);
- Yenon Levi, an Israeli tourist in 1988 (Thomas also gave undisclosed facts about this murder);
- There Johannesen in 1988 (in Norway);
- Trine Jensen in 1981; and
- Gry Storvik in 1985.

However, no physical evidence has ever been found to link Thomas to these murders, nothing but his confessions.

In 2008, Thomas withdrew all of the confessions that he previously made. His statements weren't reliable, and he clearly fabricated some of his confessions. Moreover, there were no witnesses that could place Thomas anywhere near the crime scenes.

Some say that Thomas is no more than a compulsive liar, and he had never killed anyone. Some of the victims' relatives asked to declare the trials invalid. Some professors in law and psychiatry claim that most of Thomas's confessions aren't true (if not all of them), and that he only confessed because he is mentally ill. It is also said that Thomas was under the influence of certain drugs and medication during the time of his confessions.

As of July 30, 2013, Thomas was acquitted of all

the murders that he was convicted of, but he continues to remain in a psychiatric confinement waiting for more psychiatric evaluations. The real truth about the murders lies with Thomas and victims, and may never be truly discovered.

CHAPTER 92:
THUG BEHRAM

The Thugees are a gang of professional assassins. They would travel throughout the country, join tourists and gain their confidence, and then surprise them by strangling them and taking their possessions. At one time, Thug Behram was the leader of such a group.

Thug Behram was born in the year 1765. He was of the Thugee cult, which began in India. His series of murders started when he was twenty-five years old, in the year 1790. His terror lasted for around forty years, and came to an end between the years 1830 and 1840.

According to James Paton, who was an East India Company officer working for the Thuggee and Dacoity Office in the 1830s and wrote a manuscript about the cult, Thug confessed to being present during the murders of 931 victims, and personally strangling to death around 125 to 150 persons, or maybe more.

The group consisted of twenty-five to fifty men who targeted travellers. They would kill them by strangulation, using a ceremonial cloth, a "rumal" (or handkerchief) as it is called in Hindi. A large medallion was sewn to the handkerchief. The medallion was placed on the victim's Adam's apple, and then with pressure, the victim would be strangled. After they killed their victims, the Thugees stole their possessions.

Thug was not charged or tried for his murders because he had turned King's Evidence, and he had agreed to inform on his accomplices and companions. The real number of the victims will never be accurately known because the Thugees often tried to appear as important as they could to their British captors.

CHAPTER 93:
VASILI KOMAROFF

Murder was an "an awfully easy job" to "The Wolf of Moscow" who, in the early days of Stalin, struck terror in the streets of Moscow. Although in the early 1920s the people of Russia were already living in danger from the civil war, the murders committed by "The Wolf of Moscow" were another addition to the horrors that the population had to endure.

Vasili Komaroff was born in 1871. He seemed like a happy family man, friendly and always smiling. However, he was a Dr. Jekyll and Mr. Hyde case. To the people who truly knew him and were close to the family, he was incredibly violent and abusive. On one occasion, he even tried to kill his eight-year-old son by strangulation, but due to his wife's intervention, the son lived to see another day. He dealt in the business of horses and had a stable at his home in Shabolovki district, a district in Moscow.

In 1921, the bodies of murdered men began to surface. They were discovered dumped in bags. The police started an investigation that lasted for two years. Investigators noticed that the murders, or discoveries of the bodies, always seemed to occur on Thursdays and Saturdays, the days after the selling of horses in the market. They also noticed that Vasili always attended the selling days at the market, and although he would never bring a horse with him, he would somehow always leave with a customer. The police started questioning Vasili's neighbours, and they found out about his temper and angry bursts.

One day, the police went to Vasili's house to search for illegal alcohol. That was when they found one of his victims under a stack of hay in the stable. Vasili panicked and tried to escape, but he was apprehended. Under questioning, Vasili confessed to killing about thirty-three men, but he could have killed more. Eleven of the cases were not even under investigation yet. The victims would be looking for a horse to buy, and Vasili would lure them back to his place with a promise of a better price. Once they were in the stable, he would wait for the right time before hitting his victim in the head with a hammer, or strangling him to death. His motive was robbery, although the total of money that he had stolen from his victims only equaled about $26.40, amounting to around 80 cents for each man he killed. He would then get rid of the bodies, mostly in bags. Vasili took the police to the places where he had disposed of the remaining victims. He dumped six of his victims in the Moskva River, and their remains were never found.

Vasili stated that only one man struggled, but killing everyone else was very easy. He said that he was ready to die, that he had some good times and didn't want to live anymore. In prison, Vasili tried committing suicide three times, but he failed each time. He was found guilty of all the murders, along with his wife who was considered as an accomplice because she definitely knew about her husband's crimes. They were both sentenced to death.

Vasili continued to appeal his conviction in an attempt to delay the inevitable. The courts refused to grant him an appeal, and on June 18, 1923, Vasili and his wife were both executed by a Moscow firing squad.

CHAPTER 94:
VLAD TEPES

(Count Dracula)

Vlad Tepes is the man who inspired Bram Stoker to write the character of Count Dracula, the vampire. The man actually lived centuries ago, but is still known to this day by his cruelty and the way he tortured and killed his victims. The man was known as "Dracula" which meant "the son of the devil." Vlad the Impaler's legacy still lives till today.

Vlad Tepes was born in the winter of 1431, probably in Sighişoara in Transylvania. He was the middle child between two other brothers, Mircea and Radu. His father, Vlad Dracul, gave his two younger sons to the Ottoman sultan. Vlad suffered at the hands of the Turks. The years that Vlad spent as a hostage shaped him, and he may have developed his blood thirst during these years. When Radu was released, he converted to Islam and was allowed to the Ottoman court. Vlad hated Radu and Mehmed, the future sultan.

In December 1447, Vlad II, ruler of Wallachia, and his eldest son were killed by the Hungarian John Hunyadi. The Ottoman sultan invaded Wallachia, and assigned Vlad III as ruler. However, Hunyadi invaded the country and chased Vlad away. Vlad escaped to Moldavia where he was put under his uncle's (Bogdan II) protection. In October 1451, Bodgan was assassinated, and Vlad escaped to Hungary, where he managed to impress Hunyadi by his knowledge of the Ottoman Empire, and became his advisor. After successfully invading Serbia and Wallachia, Vlad became prince of Wallachia, and he started his longest reign, from 1456 to 1462.

Vlad attempted to make the country economically stable. Although there aren't exact accounts of his actions, and there are many stories about his tortures, it is accurately known that he was a bloodthirsty cruel man. For example, he demanded honesty from his own people, and anyone who broke the law would be tortured and impaled. He killed any person, like the boyars, who threatened his reign. Vlad killed many of the Dăneşti clan members. He killed anyone who gave shelter to his rivals.

Vlad then waged a war on the Ottoman Empire, after making an alliance with the king of Hungary, Matthias Corvinus. In the winter of 1461, Vlad attacked the area between Serbia and the Black Sea, killing more than 20,000 people. Throughout his life, he killed between 20,000 and 300,000 people. He enjoyed torturing his victims. He impaled his victims and sometimes left the corpses for months. The height of the spear indicated the rank of the victim.

After this, Sultan Mehmed II invaded Wallachia and chased Vlad away to Hungary. Radu the Handsome, Vlad's younger brother, was made the new ruler. In August 1462, the new prince Radu made a deal with the king of Hungary. In Hungary, Vlad was imprisoned. It is not known when he was exactly taken captive, but the period of his captivity was not long. He was able to win back the Hungarian King's favour. It is said he married the King's cousin, although this is not certain for it is not likely for a prisoner to be permitted to marry a member of the royal family. Rumour has it he also had two sons with his new wife. He also allegedly became a member of the Catholic Church. During his time in prison, Vlad often impaled animals, torturing and mutilating birds and mice.

In 1476, Vlad re-conquered Wallachia with the help of Stefan Báthory of Transylvania, some boyars from Wallachia, and some Moldavians. A few years earlier, Radu died and was replaced by a member of the Dănești clan. Vlad was able to get the throne of Wallachia back. However, Vlad was surrounded by people who were tired of his cruelty. He had an army of less than 4,000 men. He met the Turks with this small army.

It is not accurately known how Vlad the Impaler died. Some sources state that he was killed in battle in December 1476, others claim that he was betrayed by the boyars who murdered him during the war against the Turks, or they hunted him and killed him. His head was sent to the sultan and was displayed on a stake, but the place of his grave is also unknown.

CHAPTER 95: WAYNE BODEN

In the late 1960s and early 1970s, bodies began emerging in Canada. The victims were females, and had weird bite marks on their breasts. They were raped, and had blood sucked out. It was the work of "The Vampire Rapist."

Wayne Clifford Boden was born in the year 1948, and raised in Dundas, Ontario. He spent his high school years in Glendale Secondary School in Hamilton, Ontario. This was in the early- to mid-1960s. He seemed like a normal guy to others, always smiling and charming. Not much is known about his childhood or early life, but his actions in his early twenties would make him recognizable.

Wayne's first victim was Shirley Audette. On October 3, 1969, she was discovered murdered at the rear portion of her apartment complex. Curiously, there was no proof that she struggled to save herself. It seemed that Shirley might have been looking for a new sexual experience, "rough sex." However, the experience obviously went wrong. She was raped, strangled, and had violent bite marks on her breasts. Surprisingly, she was found covered with clothes.

On November 23, Marielle Archambault, a jewelry dealer, went out with a charming man known as "Bill." When she didn't come to work the next day, her boss went to her home to check on her. She was discovered dead. The same bite marks of the previous victim were on her breasts. There was also a large quantity of drawn out blood on the floor. She had been raped and choked to death. Again, there were no signs of struggle, and she was fully clothed.

On January 16, 1970, twenty-four-year-old Jean Wray's boyfriend came to her apartment to pick her up for a scheduled date. When she didn't answer his call, he decided to go home and come back later. An hour passed, and the boyfriend came back. He found her dead, half nude body in her home. However, this time there were signs of a fight and investigators found skin cells under Jean's fingernails. Her breasts were intact. Police believed that the murderer was in her apartment when the boyfriend first knocked on the door and startled, he ran away without completing his ritual. Jean had been raped and strangled to death.

These first three murders occurred in Montreal. The fourth and final victim was in Calgary, 2,500 miles from Montreal. On May 18, 1971, thirty-three-year-old teacher Elizabeth Anne Porteous did not show up for school. Her employer called her apartment manager, and she was found dead. Again, there were clear evidences of struggle. She fought her attacker so violently that one of his cufflinks was torn off and found under her body. She was raped, strangled, and had bites on her mutilated breasts.

The investigators went on questioning Elizabeth's friends. They found out that she had been out with an attractive young man named "Bill" who had a blue coloured Mercedes. The next day, an officer found the car parked close to the crime scene. "Bill" was arrested and brought in to the station. When presented with the cufflink, the man hesitated but confirmed that he was the owner of the car, and that he was with Elizabeth a few hours before she was murdered, but he had left her unharmed.

After several hours of interrogation, the police found out that "Bill" was actually Wayne Borden. Then, Wayne confessed to the killing of Elizabeth as well as the three other killings in Montreal. However, he claimed that he had nothing to do with the murder of Norma Vaillancourt, a twenty-one-year-old woman who had been killed on July 23, 1968, and whom "The Vampire Rapist" was suspected of killing. As it turned out, a man named Raymond Suave was found guilty for that murder years later, and received a sentence of ten years in prison.

CHAPTER 96: WESTLEY ALLAN DODD

Six-year-old James went to the theatre's bathroom. A man followed. A few minutes later, everyone there heard the boy's screams. The man came out of the bathroom stall, grabbing the boy, urging him to calm down as if he was his father. "Calm down, son," he said. The man took James to his car outside, but James was able to free himself and run back to the theatre's owners screaming, "that man was going to hurt me!" The boyfriend of James's mother, William, ran after the man, tied him up, and brought him back to the theatre where they waited for the police.

Westley Allan Dodd was born on July 3, 1961, in Washington. He had two younger siblings. His parents, Jim and Carol, were constantly fighting, and had neglected him emotionally. At age thirteen, he began exposing himself to the neighbourhood children from his bedroom window while hiding his face. When he realized that that might get him in trouble, he started bicycling through the neighbourhood and exposing himself in a "safer" way to children ten years old or younger.

After his parents' divorce, and at the age of fourteen, Westley began molesting children. He first started with his cousins, the kids of a woman his father was dating, and later with other neighbourhood kids. Westley would look for jobs where he could be around kids. He would gain their trust, and then molest them while making them think that his actions were something natural. He was arrested many times for exposing himself, but never served jail time; instead, he was ordered to attend counseling.

In September of 1981, he enlisted in the Navy. He continued molesting kids, this time using money to lure them. He was then discharged from the Navy for trying to molest a young boy, and spent nineteen days in jail. After that, nothing would stop him from molesting children. He continued to choose residences and jobs that would allow him to be close to kids. In 1986, he moved to Seattle. He decided he wouldn't take no for an answer even if he had to use force. He started fantasizing about murdering his victims.

On September 4, 1989, a few days after Labor Day weekend, Westley went to David Douglas Park looking for a victim. He was able to lure William Neer (age ten) and his brother, Cole (age eleven) into a secluded area. There, he molested the boys. William escaped and managed to run towards the road, so Westley stabbed Cole, and went after William. He was able to catch up with him, and he stabbed him too. William was found barely alive. Their father was searching for them, and the police found out that there was a second boy. Cole was found dead where Westley had left him. William died at the hospital. The people of Vancouver were terrified.

After knowing that the police didn't have any solid clues, Westley began fantasizing and planning his next kill. After many failed attempts, he found his next victim on October 29. That day, Lee Iseli (age four), his brother, and a friend all went to the school playground. Westley was there, "hunting," and was able to lure a hesitant Lee away from the others. He took him to his apartment, where he molested him over and over, while taking notes in his diary and taking pictures. The next day, in the morning before going to work, Westley strangled Lee. He put him in the closet, and after work, he dumped his body. Westley was cruel and cold. The police still didn't have any solid leads.

After that, Westley decided that he would kidnap a kid at the movies. That was when he attempted to kidnap James, but instead was captured. After questioning, Westley confessed to the murders, and police found it disturbing how he enjoyed talking about it. He was charged with first-degree murder, and in January 1990, he pleaded guilty (after initially pleading not guilty). He read a statement in which he confessed that his murders were premeditated. On January 5, 1993, Westley was executed by hanging.

CHAPTER 97:
WILLIAM GEORGE
BONIN

aka the Freeway Killer

On February 23, 1996, the state of California used the lethal injection for the first time as a mean of execution. The criminal waiting to meet his fate was the "Freeway Killer."

William George Bonin was born on January 8, 1947, in Connecticut. His father was a gambler and an alcoholic. His mother also abused alcohol. Their mother eventually left William and his brother with their grandfather even though he was a convicted child molester.

At the age of eight, William was put in a juvenile hall for stealing license plates. There, older boys sexually abused him. Future psychiatric evaluation showed that William repressed the memories of ever being molested. When he returned home, William took up the practice of fondling other children.

In 1965, William joined the army and was sent to war in Vietnam. He logged 700 hours of combat. He was a good soldier and once risked his life to save another soldier. It wasn't until he was honourably discharged that it was discovered William had sexually assaulted two other soldiers at gunpoint.

In 1969, William was accused of sexually assaulting five boys in Los Angeles. He spent five years in the state hospital. In 1975, William picked up David McVicker (age fourteen), drove him to a secluded area, and raped him. He tried to choke him but then stopped and apologized, the last time that he would ever show regret. William's later victims weren't so lucky. David did go to the police, and William served three years in prison.

After a record mix-up error, he was released back into public, free to commit more crimes. This is when he vowed that he would never spend time behind bars again.

On May 28, 1979, William committed his first murder, the murder of Thomas Glen Lundgren (age thirteen). The boy was found emasculated, beaten on the face and the head, stabbed, strangled, and with his throat slashed. William had teamed up with another killer, Vernon Butts, for this murder. Together the two would go on to commit additional murders together.

August 5, 1979 is the day when Marcus Grabs (age seventeen), an exchange student from Germany, was last seen. He was sodomized, stabbed, and strangled to death. Both William and Vernon were involved. Three weeks later, Donald Hyden (age fifteen) was found dead. He was raped, mutilated, strangled to death, had his throat slashed, and there was an attempt to castrate him. The next victim was David Murillo (age seventeen) who disappeared on September 12. He was sodomized, strangled, and had his head bashed. The killings would then stop until December of the same year, when Frank Fox (age seventeen) was found murdered in the same way the others were killed.

The body count was getting higher and higher. On February 3, 1980, William and a new accomplice, Gregory Matthew Miley, picked up Charles Miranda (age fifteen). Charles was sodomized by William, and sexually assaulted with a blunt object by Gregory. Then, William strangled him with his own shirt. James McCab (age twelve) was next. The two assaulted him and also strangled him with his shirt. William would go on to kill seven more victims between March and April 1980.

On June 2, 1980, William and a third accomplice, James Munro, picked up Steven Wells (age nineteen). They all went back to the apartment for sex. They sexually assaulted Steven, strangled him, and went to dump his body.

In May 1980, the police stopped William Pugh, a seventeen-year-old thief who allegedly was present with William and witnessed one murder. Pugh, in exchange for a plea deal, told the police about William being the Freeway Killer. Police started searching for William, and put him under surveillance.

On June 11, William picked up a fifteen-year-old boy in his van. The police arrested him while he was sodomizing the boy. They found a scrapbook about the Freeway Killer in the van, along with tape and rope used on the victims. His accomplices were later arrested.

William confessed to raping and murdering twenty-one boys, but the police suspected there may have been as many as fifteen additional victims. On November 5, 1981, he was brought to trial and charged with twelve murders. After almost seventeen years of appeals, on February 23, 1996, William was executed by lethal injection.

CHAPTER 98: YANG XINHAI

"*When I killed people I had a desire. This inspired me to kill more. I don't care whether they deserve to live or not. It is none of my concern...I have no desire to be part of society. Society is not my concern.*" These words were said by China's most inexhaustible serial killer, Yang Xinhai, in order to provide a motive for his gruesome killings: he just enjoyed it and wanted to hurt society.

Yang Xinhai was born on July 29, 1968. He had three older siblings. His family was very poor. Yang was also known as Yang Zhiya, Yang Liu, and Wang Ganggang. According to his family, Yang was a bright student, but he also was an introvert. At age seventeen, Yang left his high school and his home to travel all over China, working at different jobs. Yang had a notebook in which he would right down ideas of crimes for stories and movies that he wanted to write.

Yang was punished twice to spend some time in labour camps for his theft acts in Shijiazhuang, Hebei, and in Xi'an, Shaanxi, in the years 1988 and 1991. After five years, Yang's crimes began evolving. He was sentenced to five years of imprisonment for attempting a rape in the city of Henan, but he was discharged in 1999. Yang had a girlfriend at that time that left him after learning about his criminal past. Some say that being left by his girlfriend was the reason why Yang turned on society and started committing a series of murders that would go on for years.

The killings committed by Yang occurred in four different provinces in China: Anhui, Shandong, Hebei, and Henan. He mostly killed farmers in isolated houses. He would wipe out entire families. Yang found families to target, waited until nightfall, and broke in while the families were asleep. He would kill the husband and children first, and then rape the women. He used axes, shovels, and hammers to bludgeon his victims to death. He is suspected to have killed sixty-seven victims. Yang would wear new clothes every time and larger shoes to evade the police. He would leave his victims in gruesome ways for the neighbours to discover.

In October of 2002, Yang broke into the home of a family where he killed the husband and his six-year-old daughter. The wife was pregnant, but that did not stop Yang from raping her. Although the woman suffered severe head injuries, she survived to report the crime, and a case was opened.

On November 3, 2003, the police were on a routine check of the entertainment venue in Cangzhou. Yang was present, and he was acting suspiciously. The police arrested him. They later found out that Yang had a warrant issued in his name in the four Chinese provinces. After his capture, the media turned its attention to the murders that happened, and they started to call Yang "The Monster Killer."

Under questioning, Yang confessed to twenty-three rapes, five attacks causing severe injuries, and sixty-five murders:

- In Henan, he committed seventeen rapes, five attacks, and forty-nine murders;
- In Hebei, he committed three rapes and eight murders;
- In Anhui, he committed two rapes and six murders; and
- In Shandong, he committed one rape, and two murders.

In addition, the police were able to match his DNA to many crime scenes. After some time, it was found that one of the victims gave Yang HIV.

Yang's trial began on February 1, 2004. He was found guilty for twenty-three rapes and sixty-seven murders. The trial was kept closed to protect the identities of the women raped. After less than one hour, the Luohe City Intermediary People's Court in Henan sentenced him to death. He is the most prolific, gruesome, serial killer with the longest killing spree in the history of modern China. On February 4, 2004, Yang was executed by a firing squad.

CHAPTER 99: YOO YOUNG-CHUL

One of the most notorious and horrific Korean serial killer and cannibal says, *"I may have the devil inside me."* I suspect he was correct in making that comment.

Yoo Young-Chul was born in a blue-collar family in Waha, a place near Gochang County in the north Cheolla province. He was born on April 18, 1970. He was an unexpected baby and was bought up by his grandmother. At an early age, he came into terms with the fact that his mother never really wanted to have him. When he was six, he moved up to Seoul to live with his father, two older brothers, and a younger sister. A few years later, his father married. Due to the stepmother's stiff behaviour, at the age of eight, Yoo and his younger sister ran away from home. Yoo attended the Seoul Gongdeok Elementary School, where he was teased and insulted for his poverty-stricken life.

Yoo was fond of arts and one could easily find many marks on his hands from drawing on them. He wanted to specialize in the arts, but failed to get into a good school, instead ending up at a technical high school in 1987. While he was in his second year of school, he was charged with stealing a guitar and a Sony cassette player from a neighbour's house. It was his first crime and visit to the juvenile detention centre. He never did complete graduation from the technical school.

In 1991, he met Ms. Hwang, who was a masseuse by profession. He knew and believed that she was the right woman to marry and they did just that on December 23, 1993. Unfortunately, the happier times in his life did not last too long. The property owner increased the rent where they lived and they found it difficult financially. In order to make up for their shortcomings, he tried to steal from a store, and was caught by the security guard.

Between 1995 and 1998, he was arrested several times for selling illegal pornography, theft, forgery, and identity theft. His petty crimes escalated and in 2000, he was arrested for raping a fifteen-year-old girl. Because of this, his wife divorced him in 2002, after which he served his two-year sentence in the Jeonju detention centre. He was also barred from any visitation rights to his son.

Like most serial killers, Yoo practiced his violence on dogs and other small animals. He clubbed a number of stray dogs and bashed them to death to perfect his method of murder. His weapon of choice was a hammer that he had made himself. In addition, his victims needed to meet a certain criteria and he followed a certain process for killing. Yoo always choose a house that was two stories with open courtyards and no security systems installed. These were the soft targets for Yoo. He went after wealthy and elderly families because of the jealously he felt on the notion of a harmonious family.

He would climb over the fence and find a way into the house. Yoo was a planned killer who before taking any step would closely observe the movements that were going on in the house. After he knew no one was watching, he would get inside with a six-inch blade and his handmade hammer. After each brutal killing, he would systematically wipe out all the traces of the crime. Unlike other killers, Yoo used a special kind of gloves and shoes, which did not leave any markings on the floor.

In 2003, Yoo found a new girl, who was an escort by profession. She later found out about Yoo's list of crimes and broke up with him. He soon developed hatred towards all prostitutes and decided to kill escort girls as revenge. He would call the sex parlours and ask the girls to come down to his apartment. When they arrived, he would never have any physical contact as he feared of being caught by the DNA samples found. He would smash their heads with a hammer and drag the body in the bathroom to mutilate it. Yoo made sure to scrape off the skin at fingers and cut down the nails as to leave no evidence behind. He would mutilate the dead bodies and consume the liver and the brain. Yoo believed that consuming both the liver and brain would result in keeping his mind and body fit. He would dump their bodies at a construction site or subway near his house.

He murdered twenty-one people, which included old rich women and prostitutes. Yoo Young-Chul is also known as a cannibal killer as he had confessed to eating the liver of the victims killed. He committed these crimes between September 2003 and July 2004, after which he was arrested and tried.

He was found guilty for twenty of the killings, though one of the cases was not tried due to technicalities. He was sentenced to death in 2004, and is currently on death row.

CHAPTER 100:
ZHOU KEHUA

If talking about the most hated killers in China, then Zhou Kehua would have been surely on the list. Zhou Kehua was a Chinese robber and serial killer. He was an A-level fugitive, who was wanted by the Ministry of Public Security. He was also known as the bank killer, as most of the crimes he committed were near banks.

Zhou was born on February 6, 1970, in a small town named Jinkou near the Shapingba District. He committed his first crime in 1985, at the young age of fifteen. Zhou was sentenced to jail for fourteen days under the charges of molestation. Over the next five years, he had other run-ins with the law for burglary and illegal possession of weapons. In the year 1991, he was again arrested and sentenced to a re-education through labour camp for illegal possession of firearms.

Zhou met a girl named Zhang Guiying at a massage parlour in Yibin where she had been working. He became one of Zhang's regular customers. After his death, twenty-year-old Zhang was charged with helping her boyfriend hide when he was on the run and also helping him hide stolen money. Zhou had no moral struggle in his mind because he always knew at the end he would get a death sentence one way or another.

Below is a timeline of his killings:

- On April 22, 2004, he committed a bank robbery of 70,000 Yuan, approximately $11,300 USD. During the robbery, one woman was killed and another was injured.
- On May 16, 2005, two suspects shot and robbed a couple near a bank in Shapingba district in Chongqing. A witness to the incident was also shot, leaving all the three dead. The robbers fled with 170,000 Yuan.
- On March 19, 2009, an eighteen-year-old solider named Han Juniang of the People's Liberation Army was killed. The soldier, who was on duty outside a garrison in Chongqing, was shot twice in the chest with a pistol. From the crime scene, the suspect ran with the guard's submachine gun.
- On October 14, 2009, he shot a fifty-six-year-old farmer with a homemade gun in a park in Tianxin located in Changsha (Hunan Province).
- On December 24, 2009, a forty-one-year-old man was fired at when he was walking towards his car carrying 45,000 Yuan he had just withdrawn from the bank. He was shot in the head and died at the scene.
- On October 25, 2010, in the Yuhua district of Changsha, he gunned down a man who ran a trading company.
- On June 28, 2011, a forty-eight-year-old businessperson was shot twice in the head and once in the stomach near a construction

spot in Tianxin. The killer fled and the businessman was rushed to the hospital.

- On January 6, 2012, a forty-five-year-old man was shot and robbed in Nanjing, Jiangsu province. He was shot after withdrawing 200,000 Yuan from a bank in the Xiaguan district. The suspect fled the scene by jumpstarting a vehicle. The businessman died on the spot.
- On Aug 10, 2012, a woman was shot dead and two others were injured in front of a bank in the Shapingba district in Chongqing.

In total, Kehua stole about 250,000 Yuan from all the robberies. He also killed a railway police officer while he was on duty patrolling a section of railway.

A manhunt was initiated by the Chinese police officials to capture the most cold-blooded bank murderer in history. A sum of 5.4 million Yuan was offered in reward for helping the police officials capture or locate him. On August 14, 2012, Kehua was gunned down by the police in Ertang Village, Chongqing.

There is still much controversy involved in the whole story. Despite repeated affirmations by the Chongqing authorities, many local people are still suspicious. They believe that the person who was killed was not Zhou Kehua, but a policeman in plain clothes.

CHAPTER 101: LONG ISLAND SERIAL KILLER

BY JJ SLATE

In 2010, police began searching remote areas near Long Island Beach in hopes of finding Shannan Gilbert, a missing escort who was last seen running screaming from an unknown assailant in the middle of the night. What they would find over the next year and a half during their search would rock the beach town community to its core. Remains of ten individuals, eight of them women, one male, and one female toddler, were discovered in marshy areas spread out along three counties along Gilgo Beach, Oak Beach, and Jones Beach State Park.

In November 2011, police announced they believed that one individual was responsible for all ten murders. Word came later that they were also considering an additional four other cases involving victims previously discovered in coastal areas of New York to determine if they might also be connected to the same killer.

The identified victims in the original ten include five young women in their twenties that had been reported missing between 2005 and 2010: Jessica Taylor, Maureen Brainard-Barnes, Melissa Barthelemy, Megan Waterman, and Amber Lynn Costello. All five victims had been using Craigslist to advertise their escort and prostitution services.

Melissa Barthelemy's teenage sister later told the media that the killer had used her sister's cell phone to call her several times and taunt her. Melissa disappeared in July of 2009, but her sister, Amanda, received at least seven disturbing and vulgar phone calls from a man using Melissa's phone after the disappearance. In the final call, he admitted that he had killed Melissa, crushing the family's hopes of ever finding her alive. Melissa's body was one of the first to be discovered in December of 2010. Police traced the calls from the victim's cell phone and determined they were originating from the Manhattan Times Square area.

The five unidentified remains include an Asian male wearing woman's clothing, who likely worked as a prostitute at the time of his death. He was killed with violent blows to the head, unlike the other murder victims who were likely strangled. Also discovered were a mother and her toddler daughter. Another set of remains was connected to a pair of legs that had been discovered in a plastic bag nearly a decade earlier on Fire Island. A final unidentified female victim was also linked to the other victims, after her head, right foot, and hands were located. The rest of her body had been discovered in 2000, near the area where Jessica Taylor's remains were later found.

Shannan Gilbert's remains were eventually found in a marsh in 2011, nineteen months after the search for her began. Despite the fact that Shannan was an escort who advertised her services on Craigslist, just like the five identified victims, police don't believe she was killed by the same person as the other victims. They suggest that she was running from someone in the dark, and may have stumbled into the thick marsh and drowned. Shannan's family vehemently disagrees with this conclusion and insists that she is the eleventh victim.

Police have released little information about what they know about the killer, dubbed by some as the Long Island Serial Killer or the Gilgo Beach Killer, but what we do know is terrifying. The ten victims were murdered between the years 1996 and 2010. It is clear that the killer targets prostitutes in the Long Island area, likely soliciting their services from Craigslist. While it is difficult to pinpoint cause of death in most of the victims, police believe that the majority of the women were likely strangled and then dismembered. Several of the victims were disposed of in burlap sacks or plastic bags.

In April of 2011, *The New York Times* reported it is likely the serial killer is a white male between the ages of twenty-five and forty-five. FBI profilers and serial killer experts believe he may even be married or have a stable girlfriend. He is probably an educated and well-spoken individual. He is employed, financially secure, and possibly works at a job that would give him access to burlap sacks, such as landscaping, contracting, or fishing.

Some believe that the killer may be an ex-cop who is familiar with investigative techniques. The taunting calls that were made to Melissa Barthelemy's sister were all traced to crowded areas in the city where surveillance video would be useless. The killer also kept the calls under three minutes, indicating he may have known it takes between three and five minutes to trace a call. In addition, the killer took the time to dismember and dispose of his earliest victims in a scrupulous manner, perhaps indicating some knowledge that this course of action would hinder the investigation.

Other FBI profilers and serial killer experts suspect the killer may be a seasonal vacationer to the Long Island area. Since the five identified victims all went missing in the summer months, it is possible the killer has his own vacation home or visits his parents' home in the area each year. Many believe the locations of the disposal sites indicate his familiarity with the area. It is possible the killer grew up in the Long Island area and returns each summer.

Are any of these assumptions about the killer true? We won't know anything until the police solve the decades old mystery and bring an end to his reign of terror. Until then, the collective community of Long Island waits with bated breath.

Author's note: This final bonus case file was written by up-and-coming true crime writer, JJ Slate. JJ's debut true crime book, Missing Wives, Missing Lives, *a chilling collection of true cases in which a wife has mysteriously vanished, presumably at the hands of her husband, released June 16, 2014 and quickly became an Amazon bestseller in several categories.*

For more details about JJ and her books, please visit any of the following sites:

Website

www.jenniferjslate.com

Facebook

www.facebook.com/jjslate

Twitter

www.twitter.com/jenniferjslate

BOOKS BY RJ PARKER

Parents Who Killed Their Children: True Stories of Filicide, Mental Health and Postpartum Psychosis

Serial Homicide: Notorious Serial Killers: (4 Books in Series)

Abduction

Top Cases of the FBI: Volumes I and II

The Basement

The Staircase

Forensic Analysis and DNA in Criminal Investigations and Cold Cases Solved: True Crime Stories

Serial Killers Encyclopedia: The Encyclopedia of Serial Killers from A to Z

Social Media Monsters: Killers Who Target Victims on the Internet

Escaped Killer

Revenge Killings

Killing the Rainbow

Marc Lépine: True Story of the Montreal Massacre: School Shootings

Backseat Tragedies: Hot Car Deaths

Women Who Kill

Beyond Stick and Stones

Cold Blooded Killers

Case Closed: Serial Killers Captured

Radical Islamic Terrorism in America Today

Hell's Angels Biker War

Serial Killer Groupies

Serial Killer Case Files

Blood Money: The Method and Madness of Assassins: Stories of Real Contract Killers

Serial Killers True Crime Anthologies: Volumes 1 – 4

ABOUT THE
AUTHOR

RJ Parker, Ph.D., is an award-winning and bestselling true crime author and owner of RJ Parker Publishing, Inc. He has written over 30 true crime books which are available in eBook, paperback and audiobook editions and have sold in over 100 countries. He holds certifications in Serial Crime, Criminal Profiling and a Ph.D. in Criminology.

To date, RJ has donated over 3,000 autographed books to allied troops serving overseas and to our wounded warriors recovering in Naval and Army hospitals all over the world. He also donates to Victims of Violent Crimes Canada.

CONTACT INFORMATION

Author's Email:

AuthorRJParker@gmail.com

Publisher's Email:

Agent@RJParkerPublishing.com

Website:

http://RJPARKERPUBLISHING.com/

Twitter:

http://www.Twitter.com/realRJParker

Facebook:

https://www.Facebook.com/AuthorRJParker

Instagram:

https://Instagram.com/RJParkerPub

Bookbub:

https://www.bookbub.com/authors/rj-parker

Amazon Author's Page:

rjpp.ca/RJ-PARKER-BOOKS

REFERENCES

Much of the content in this book was gleaned from many contacts, including the following. Special thanks to:

Murderpedia The Encyclopedia of Murderers
Crime Library and Turner Entertainment
The Guardian UK
Federal Bureau of Investigation
State of Texas Supreme Court
Amarillo Police Department and several other police departments who sent me summary reports
Royal Canadian Mounted Police
Peel Police, Ontario
Toronto Police, Division 32, Ontario
Serial Killers Magazine
Huffington Post Crime

34117458R00191

Made in the USA
San Bernardino, CA
30 April 2019